I've been waiting for a book like this for a long time. At last, my dear and longtime friends, Charles and Frances Hunter, have given it to the church and to each of us.

In every book of the Bible, we get the heart of the book, the very cream. These promises come not from man, but from God Himself, in the most intimate and personal way—to both our minds and souls, yes, even to our bodies. This is really a whole-person book!

Get your *receiver* out and take in each promise. Have your *expector* out so that not one will pass you by. God's promises will change your life forever.

—Oral Roberts
Founder and Chancellor of Oral Roberts University

The promises of God have been a treasure in our lives. As we have believed and spoken the promises, God has performed them. This book will inspire you to believe for God's best.

—Billy Joe Daugherty
Victory Christian Center

If you are a Christian, you are a "promise" person! The more promises we can get a hold of, the bigger we become. Anything Frances Hunter says is always exciting, bold, and full of faith! Not only does she stand on the promises for her own family, but she is also a "promise" person for other families, including mine.

Thank God for this book to remind us again that we, too, are "promise" people.

—Marilyn Hickey

Charles and Frances have done it again. When you would have thought they told us everything, they've come around to encourage us one more time.

Every pastor should have this book on his desk. It is great for telephone and personal counseling, and an easy way to give a good word to anyone.

I promise you—no. Charles and Frances promise you—no. God promises you that this book will change you life.

—Robb Thompson
Senior Pastor, Family Harvest Church International
Tinley Park, IL

I Promise...

love, God

Given These Wonderful Promises

O Lord, you have given me these wonderful promises just because you want to be kind to me, because of your own great heart. O Lord, there is no one like you—there is no other God. In fact, we have never even heard of another god like you! (1 Chronicles 17:19–20 TLB)

I Promise…

love, God

Charles and Frances HUNTER

WHITAKER HOUSE

I PROMISE... LOVE, GOD

Charles and Frances Hunter
Hunter Ministries
P.O. Box 5600
Kingwood, TX 77325-5600
www.cfhunter.org
e-mail: wec@cfhunter.org

ISBN: 0-88368-668-6
Printed in the United States of America
© 2001 by Charles and Frances Hunter

Whitaker House
30 Hunt Valley Circle
New Kensington, PA 15068
www.whitakerhouse.com

Library of Congress Cataloging-in-Publication Data

Hunter, Charles, 1920–
I promise… love, God / by Charles and Frances Hunter.
    p.   cm.
ISBN 0-88368-668-6 (pbk. : alk. paper)
1. God—Promises—Biblical teaching. I. Hunter, Frances Gardner, 1916– II. Title.
BS680.P68 H86 2001
220.5'20816—dc21   2001002558

---

2 3 4 5 6 7 8 9 10 11 12 13 14 ⊞ 14 13 12 11 10 09 08 07 06 05 04

Contents

There has not failed one word of all
His good promise.
—1 Kings 8:56

Foreword

I'm a "promise" person!

Shortly after I was gloriously saved, at the age of forty-nine, a man walked up to me and said, "Do you know there are over seventy thousand promises in the Word of God?"

With utter amazement I said, "Really?" I had never read the Bible—the gold edge wasn't even cracked on a Bible given to me in 1924. As a result, I did not have the faintest idea the Bible was power-packed with promises. However, his statement created a hunger in me to discover what he was talking about!

Then I said, "God, let me live long enough to discover every promise You have in the Bible!" Immediately I began avidly reading the Bible, searching for promises with all my heart.

I began to devour the incredible promises and have continued to be a "promise" person all of my Christian life, continually searching in the Bible for more of those awesome promises of God! Because I have constantly stood on God's promises, my Christian life has always been so exciting.

I want to share these promises with you. In writing this book I have researched several different versions of the Bible: *New King James, Living Bible, Amplified, New International Version*, and others. From this extensive reading I have included promises from every book in the Bible, in the particular version where I think it is expressed best and will speak inspiration to your heart in the greatest way.

Don't rush through reading! Take time to absorb the promises! Take the time necessary to let each and every promise seep into your heart like a slow, soaking rain to a thirsty ground. Meditate on each promise until your hunger and thirst are satisfied.

These are actual promises made by almighty God and the Lord Jesus Christ. To receive the most from every promise, make your Bible personal and receive these promises as God speaking to you personally as you meditate on them. They will get into your very soul and spirit until you find that refreshment comes as you read the precious Word of God. God wants to manifest all the blessings He has promised in His Word.

As you read and absorb these promises, you will find that you have drawn closer to God and His precious Son, Jesus. He is actually talking to you as you read His promises. Think of your Bible reading time as a personal interview with God. He will gladly reveal His heart's desire to bless you.

Your exploration will cause you to love God and His Son more and more because they love you more than anything or anyone.

You were chosen before the foundations of the universe were laid. Before time was created, you were in His heart, and blessing you was on His mind.

You have been eternally destined to be a special person in His kingdom, regardless of your function or duty.

This book is not intended to quote every promise in the Bible. However, I believe the Holy Spirit has inspired our selection of some twelve hundred promises.

Many of the promises that you might think are just one, actually contain multiple promises. These are really "promise passages" rather than promise verses. To illustrate this fact, I have picked one at random from John 5:24–29. Although this passage is listed as only one promise, we can actually find twenty promises contained within. They are listed below.

1. *"Most assuredly,"* (without a doubt, indubitably)

2. *"I say to you,"* (He talks to us!)

3. *"he who hears My word and believes in Him who sent Me has everlasting life,"* (forever and forever)

4. *"and shall not come into judgment,"* (never, never, never)

5. *"but has passed from death into life."* (hallelujah)

6. *"Most assuredly,"* (no question about it)

7. *"I say to you,"* (I'm still talking)

8. *"the hour is coming,"* (praise God)

9. *"and now is,"* (sooner than you think)

10. *"when the dead will hear the voice of the Son of God,"* (our ears are open to His voice)

11. *"and those who hear will live."* (glory to God)

12. *"For as the Father has life in Himself,"* (He's not dead)

13. *"so He has granted the Son to have life in Himself,"* (He's alive)

14. *"and has given Him authority"* (all authority—the right to speak)

15. *"to execute judgment also,"* (plus action as well)

16. *"because He is the Son of Man."* (already proven)

17. *"Do not marvel at this; for the hour is coming in which all who are in the graves will hear His voice"* (He's speaking)

18. *"and come forth;"* (all of us)

19. *"those who have done good, to the resurrection of life,"* (praise God)

20. *"and those who have done evil, to the resurrection of condemnation."* (the choice is always ours)

To make it easy for you to locate the book in the Bible where you want to be blessed by the promises, I have not listed these in the order they are listed in the Old and New Testaments; rather, I have alphabetized the books to make it very simple for you.

I have pulled out the heart of each of the promises and put it in a caption preceding the Scripture passage so that you can easily discover the promise.

Charles says that I have skimmed the cream off the Bible and put it into a book!

Open this book.

Open your heart.

Open your expectation.

God's promises will change your life—forever!

—FRANCES HUNTER

Promises from Acts

Baptized with the Holy Spirit

And being assembled together with them, He commanded them not to depart from Jerusalem, but to wait for the Promise of the Father, "which," He said, "you have heard from Me; for John truly baptized with water, but you shall be baptized with the Holy Spirit not many days from now." (Acts 1:4–5)

You Shall Receive Power

But you shall receive power when the Holy Spirit has come upon you; and you shall be witnesses to Me in Jerusalem, and in all Judea and Samaria, and to the end of the earth. (Acts 1:8)

Will So Come in Like Manner

Behold, two men stood by them in white apparel, who also said, "Men of Galilee, why do you stand gazing up into heaven? This same Jesus, who was taken up from you into heaven, will so come in like manner as you saw Him go into heaven." (Acts 1:10–11)

Filled with the Holy Spirit

When the Day of Pentecost had fully come, they were all with one accord in one place. And suddenly there came a sound from heaven, as of a rushing mighty wind, and it filled the whole house where they were sitting. Then there appeared to them divided tongues, as of fire, and one sat upon each of them. And they were all filled with the Holy Spirit and began to speak with other tongues, as the Spirit gave them utterance. (Acts 2:1–4)

Whoever Calls Shall Be Saved

And it shall come to pass in the last days, says God, that I will pour out of My Spirit on all flesh; your sons and your daughters shall prophesy, your young men shall see visions, your old men shall dream dreams. And on My menservants and on My maidservants I will pour out My Spirit in those days; and they shall prophesy. I will show wonders in heaven above and signs in the earth beneath: blood and fire and vapor of smoke. The sun shall be turned into darkness, and the moon into blood, before the coming of the great and awesome day of the Lord. And it shall come to pass that whoever calls on the name of the Lord shall be saved. (Acts 2:17–21)

Death Could Not Keep Him in Its Grip

But you followed God's prearranged plan. With the help of lawless Gentiles, you nailed him to the cross and murdered him. However, God released him from the horrors of death and raised him back to life again for death could not keep him in its grip. (Acts 2:23–24 NLT)

This Jesus God Has Raised Up

Therefore, [David,] being a prophet, and knowing that God had sworn with an oath to him that of the fruit of his body, according to the flesh, He would raise up the Christ to sit on his throne, he, foreseeing this, spoke concerning the resurrection of the Christ, that His soul was not left in Hades, nor did His flesh see corruption. This Jesus God has raised up, of which we are all witnesses. (Acts 2:30–32)

The Gift of the Holy Spirit

"Therefore let all the house of Israel know assuredly that God has made this Jesus, whom you crucified, both LORD and Christ." Now when they heard this, they were cut to the heart, and said to Peter and the rest of the apostles, "Men and brethren, what shall we do?" Then Peter said to them, "Repent, and let every one of you be baptized in the name of Jesus Christ for the remission of sins; and you shall receive the gift of the Holy Spirit." (Acts 2:36–38)

Promise Is to You and Your Children

For the promise is to you, and to your children, and to all who are afar off, as many as the LORD our God will call. (Acts 2:39)

Times of Refreshing May Come

Repent therefore and be converted, that your sins may be blotted out, so that times of refreshing may come from the presence of the LORD. (Acts 3:19)

All the Families Shall Be Blessed

You are sons of the prophets, and of the covenant which God made with our fathers, saying to Abraham, "And in your seed all the families of the earth shall be blessed." (Acts 3:25)

Well and Sound in Body

Let it be known and understood by all of you, and by the whole house of Israel, that in the name and through the power and authority of Jesus Christ of Nazareth, Whom you crucified, [but] Whom God raised from the dead, in Him and by means of Him this man is standing here before you well and sound in body. (Acts 4:10 AMP)

By Which We Must Be Saved

Nor is there salvation in any other, for there is no other name under heaven given among men by which we must be saved. (Acts 4:12)

You Are God

Lord, You are God, who made heaven and earth and the sea, and all that is in them. (Acts 4:24)

They Spoke the Word of God with Boldness

"Now, Lord, look on their threats, and grant to Your servants that with all boldness they may speak Your word, by stretching out Your hand to heal, and that signs and wonders may be done through the name of Your holy Servant Jesus." And when they had prayed, the place where they were assembled together was shaken; and they were all filled with the Holy Spirit, and they spoke the word of God with boldness. (Acts 4:29–31)

You Cannot Overthrow It

If this plan or this work is of men, it will come to nothing; but if it is of God, you cannot overthrow it; lest you even be found to fight against God. (Acts 5:38–39)

Him You Shall Hear

The LORD your God will raise up for you a Prophet like me from your brethren. Him you shall hear. (Acts 7:37)

Earth Is My Footstool

However, the Most High does not dwell in temples made with hands, as the prophet says: "Heaven is My throne, and earth is My footstool." (Acts 7:48)

Jesus Christ Is the Son of God

And as they continued along on the way, they came to some water, and the eunuch exclaimed, See, [here is] water! What is to hinder my being baptized? And Philip said, If you believe with all your heart [if you have a conviction, full of joyful trust, that Jesus is the Messiah and accept Him as the Author of your salvation in the kingdom of God, giving Him your obedience, then] you may. And he replied, I do believe that Jesus Christ is the Son of God. (Acts 8:36–37 AMP)

God Has Cleansed

And the voice came to him again a second time, What God has cleansed and pronounced clean, do not you defile and profane by regarding and calling common and unhallowed or unclean. (Acts 10:15 AMP)

Is No Respecter of Persons

And Peter opened his mouth and said: Most certainly and thoroughly I now perceive and understand that God shows no partiality and is no respecter of persons. (Acts 10:34 AMP)

God Was with Him

God anointed Jesus of Nazareth with the Holy Spirit and with power, who went about doing good and healing all who were oppressed by the devil, for God was with Him. (Acts 10:38)

God anointed and consecrated Jesus of Nazareth with the [Holy] Spirit and with strength and ability and power; how He went about doing good and, in particular, curing all who were harassed and oppressed by [the power of] the devil, for God was with Him. (Acts 10:38 AMP)

God Raised Him Up on the Third Day

And we are witnesses of all things which He did both in the land of the Jews and in Jerusalem, whom they killed by hanging on a tree. Him God raised up on the third day, and showed Him openly. (Acts 10:39–40)

Word Multiplied

But the word of God grew and multiplied. (Acts 12:24)

God Brought Him Back to Life

When they had fulfilled all the prophecies concerning his death, he was taken from the cross and placed in a tomb. But God brought him back to life again! (Acts 13:29–30 TLB)

Freed from All Guilt

Brothers! Listen! In this man Jesus, there is forgiveness for your sins! Everyone who trusts in him is freed from all guilt and declared righteous—something the Jewish law could never do. (Acts 13:38–39 TLB)

For I Work a Work in Your Day

Behold, you despisers, marvel and perish! For I work a work in your days, a work which you will by no means believe, though one were to declare it to you. (Acts 13:41)

I Am Doing Something in Your Day

Look and perish, you despisers [of the truth], for I am doing something in your day—something that you won't believe when you hear it announced. (Acts 13:41 TLB)

The Lord Who Does All These Things

After this I will return and will rebuild the tabernacle of David, which has fallen down; I will rebuild its ruins, and I will set it up; so that the rest of mankind may seek the LORD, even all the Gentiles who are called by My name, says the LORD who does all these things. (Acts 15:16–17)

Believe on the Lord Jesus Christ

So they said, "Believe on the LORD Jesus Christ, and you will be saved, you and your household." (Acts 16:31)

For We Are Also His Offspring

The God Who produced and formed the world and all things in it, being LORD of heaven and earth, does not dwell in handmade shrines. Neither is He served by human hands, as though He lacked anything, for it is He Himself Who gives life and breath and all things to all [people]. And He made from one [common origin, one source, one blood] all nations of men to settle on the face of the earth, having definitely determined [their] allotted periods of time and the fixed boundaries of their habitation (their settlements, lands, and abodes) so that they should seek God, in the hope that they might feel after Him and find Him, although He is not far from each one of us. For in Him we live and move and have our being; as even some of your [own] poets have said, For we are also His offspring. (Acts 17:24–28 AMP)

Unusual Miracles

Now God worked unusual miracles by the hands of Paul, so that even handkerchiefs or aprons were brought from his body to the sick, and the diseases left them and the evil spirits went out of them. (Acts 19:11–12)

More Blessed to Give

I have shown you in every way, by laboring like this, that you must support the weak. And remember the words of the LORD Jesus, that He said, "It is more blessed to give than to receive." (Acts 20:35)

Promises from Amos

Revealing His Secret

Surely the Lord God will do nothing without revealing His secret to His servants the prophets.

(Amos 3:7 AMP)

God Is His Name

For behold, He Who forms the mountains and creates the wind and declares to man what is his thought, Who makes the morning darkness and treads on the heights of the earth—the Lord, the God of hosts, is His name!

(Amos 4:13 AMP)

The Days Are Coming

Behold, the days are coming, says the Lord, that the plowman shall overtake the reaper, and the treader of grapes him who sows the seed; and the mountains shall drop sweet wine and all the hills shall melt [that is, everything heretofore barren and unfruitful shall overflow with spiritual blessing]. And I will bring back the exiles of My people Israel, and they shall build the waste cities and inhabit them; and they shall plant vineyards and drink the wine from them; they shall also make gardens and eat the fruit of them. And I will plant them upon their land, and they shall no more be torn up out of their land which I gave them, says the Lord your God.

(Amos 9:13–15 AMP)

Promises from 1 Chronicles

Strength and Gladness

For the LORD is great and greatly to be praised; He is also to be feared above all gods. For all the gods of the peoples are idols, but the LORD made the heavens. Honor and majesty are before Him; strength and gladness are in His place. (1 Chronicles 16:25–27)

Given These Wonderful Promises

O Lord, you have given me these wonderful promises just because you want to be kind to me, because of your own great heart. O Lord, there is no one like you—there is no other God. In fact, we have never even heard of another god like you! (1 Chronicles 17:19–20 TLB)

Not Leave You or Forsake You

Be strong and of good courage, and do it; do not fear nor be dismayed, for the LORD God; my God; will be with you. He will not leave you nor forsake you, until you have finished all the work for the service of the house of the LORD . (1 Chronicles 28:20)

Give Strength to All

Yours, O LORD, is the greatness, the power and the glory, the victory and the majesty; for all that is in heaven and in earth is Yours; Yours is the kingdom, O LORD, and You are exalted as head over all. Both riches and honor come from You, and You reign over all. In Your hand is power and might; in Your hand it is to make great and to give strength to all. (1 Chronicles 29:11–12)

Promises from 2 Chronicles

Glory of the Lord Filled the House of God

And when they lifted up their voice with the trumpets and cymbals and instruments of music, and praised the LORD, saying: "For He is good, for His mercy endures forever," that the house, the house of the LORD, was filled with a cloud, so that the priests could not continue ministering because of the cloud; for the glory of the LORD filled the house of God. (2 Chronicles 5:13–14)

To Show Himself Strong

For the eyes of the LORD run to and fro throughout the whole earth, to show Himself strong on behalf of those whose heart is loyal to Him. (2 Chronicles 16:9)

The Battle Is Not Yours, but God's

Thus says the LORD to you: "Do not be afraid nor dismayed because of this great multitude, for the battle is not yours, but God's." (2 Chronicles 20:15)

Mercy Endures Forever

Praise the LORD, for His mercy endures forever. (2 Chronicles 20:21)

God Made Him Prosper

As long as [Uzziah] sought the LORD, God made him prosper. (2 Chronicles 26:5)

God Will Not Turn His Face from You

For if you return to the LORD, your brethren and your children will be treated with compassion by those who lead them captive, so that they may come back to this land; for the LORD your God is gracious and merciful, and will not turn His face from you if you return to Him. (2 Chronicles 30:9)

Promises from Colossians

Great Peace

May God our Father shower you with blessings and fill you with his great peace.

(Colossians 1:2 TLB)

Good News Changed Yours

Whenever we pray for you we always begin by giving thanks to God the Father of our Lord Jesus Christ, for we have heard how much you trust the Lord, and how much you love his people. And you are looking forward to the joys of heaven, and have been ever since the Gospel first was preached to you. The same Good News that came to you is going out all over the world and changing lives everywhere, just as it changed yours that very first day you heard it and understood about God's great kindness to sinners.

(Colossians 1:3–6 TLB)

He Rescued Us

And always thankful to the Father who has made us fit to share all the wonderful things that belong to those who live in the kingdom of light. For he has rescued us out of the darkness and gloom of Satan's kingdom and brought us into the kingdom of his dear Son, who bought our freedom with his blood and forgave us all our sins. (Colossians 1:12–14 TLB)

Redemption

In whom we have redemption through His blood, the forgiveness of sins. (Colossians 1:14)

In Him All Things Consist

For by Him all things were created that are in heaven and that are on earth, visible and invisible, whether thrones or dominions or principalities or powers. All things were created through Him and for Him. And He is before all things, and in Him all things consist. (Colossians 1:16–17)

Nothing Left against You

It was through what his Son did that God cleared a path for everything to come to him—all things in heaven and on earth—for Christ's death on the cross has made peace with God for all by his blood. This includes you who were once so far away from God. You were his enemies and hated him and were separated from him by your evil thoughts and actions, yet now he has brought you back as his friends. He has done this through the death on the cross of his own human body, and now as a result Christ has brought you into the very presence of God, and you are standing there before him with nothing left against you—nothing left that he could even chide you for. (Colossians 1:20–22 TLB)

Holy and Blameless

And you, who once were alienated and enemies in your mind by wicked works, yet now He has reconciled in the body of His flesh through death, to present you holy, and blameless, and above reproach in His sight; if indeed you continue in the faith, grounded and steadfast, and are not moved away from the hope of the gospel which you heard, which was preached to every creature under heaven, of which I, Paul, became a minister.   (Colossians 1:21–23)

Christ in Your Hearts

He has kept this secret for centuries and generations past, but now at last it has pleased him to tell it to those who love him and live for him, and the riches and glory of his plan are for you Gentiles too. And this is the secret: that Christ in your hearts is your only hope of glory.   (Colossians 1:26 TLB)

Christ in You

To them God willed to make known what are the riches of the glory of this mystery among the Gentiles: which is Christ in you, the hope of glory.   (Colossians 1:27)

Christ's Mighty Energy

This is my work, and I can do it only because Christ's mighty energy is at work within me.   (Colossians 1:29 TLB)

Untapped Treasures

In him lie hidden all the mighty, untapped treasures of wisdom and knowledge. (Colossians 2:3 TLB)

You Have Everything When You Have Christ

For in Christ there is all of God in a human body; so you have everything when you have Christ, and you are filled with God through your union with Christ. He is the highest Ruler, with authority over every other power. When you came to Christ he set you free from your evil desires, not by a bodily operation of circumcision but by a spiritual operation, the baptism of your souls. For in baptism you see how your old, evil nature died with him and was buried with him; and then you came up out of death with him into a new life because you trusted the Word of the mighty God who raised Christ from the dead.

(Colossians 2:9–12 TLB)

Gave You a Share

You were dead in sins, and your sinful desires were not yet cut away. Then he gave you a share in the very life of Christ, for he forgave all your sins, and blotted out the charges proved against you, the list of his commandments which you had not obeyed. He took this list of sins and destroyed it by nailing it to Christ's cross. In this way God took away Satan's power to accuse you of sin, and God openly displayed to the whole world Christ's triumph at the cross where your sins were all taken away.

(Colossians 2:13–15 TLB)

Your Real Life Is in Heaven

Since you became alive again, so to speak, when Christ arose from the dead, now set your sights on the rich treasures and joys of heaven where he sits beside God in the place of honor and power. Let heaven fill your thoughts; don't spend your time worrying about things down here. You should have as little desire for this world as a dead person does. Your real life is in heaven with Christ and God. And when Christ who is our real life comes back again, you will shine with him and share in all his glories.

(Colossians 3:1–4 TLB)

He Is Equally Available to All

You are living a brand new kind of life that is continually learning more and more of what is right, and trying constantly to be more and more like Christ who created this new life within you. In this new life one's nationality or race or education or social position is unimportant; such things mean nothing. Whether a person has Christ is what matters, and he is equally available to all.

(Colossians 3:10–11 TLB)

Your Responsibility and Privilege

Let the peace of heart which comes from Christ be always present in your hearts and lives, for this is your responsibility and privilege as members of his body. And always be thankful.   (Colossians 3:15 TLB)

From the Lord You Will Receive the Reward

And whatever you do, do it heartily, as to the Lord and not to men, knowing that from the Lord you will receive the reward of the inheritance; for you serve the Lord Christ.   (Colossians 3:23)

Promises from 1 Corinthians

Called to Be Saints

To those who are sanctified in Christ Jesus, called to be saints, with all who in every place call on the name of Jesus Christ our Lord, both theirs and ours: Grace to you and peace from God our Father and the Lord Jesus Christ.   (1 Corinthians 1:2–3)

He Always Does Just What He Says

He has enriched your whole life. He has helped you speak out for him and has given you a full understanding of the truth; what I told you Christ could do for you has happened! Now you have every grace and blessing; every spiritual gift and power for doing his will are yours during this time of waiting for the return of our Lord Jesus Christ. And he guarantees right up to the end that you will be counted free from all sin and guilt on that day when he returns. God will surely do this for you, for he always does just what he says, and he is the one who invited you into this wonderful friendship with his Son, even Christ our Lord. (1 Corinthians 1:5–9 TLB)

Ever True to His Promise

God is faithful (reliable, trustworthy, and therefore ever true to His promise, and He can be depended on); by Him you were called into companionship and participation with His Son, Jesus Christ our Lord. (1 Corinthians 1:9 AMP)

The Power of God

For Christ did not send me to baptize, but to preach the gospel, not with wisdom of words, lest the cross of Christ should be made of no effect. For the message of the cross is foolishness to those who are perishing, but to us who are being saved it is the power of God. (1 Corinthians 1:17–18)

For Christ (the Messiah) sent me out not to baptize but [to evangelize by] preaching the glad tidings (the Gospel), and that not with verbal eloquence, lest the cross of Christ should be deprived of force and emptied of its power and rendered vain (fruitless, void of value and of no effect). For the story and message of the cross is sheer absurdity and folly to those who are perishing and on their way to perdition, but to us who are being saved it is the [manifestation of] the power of God. (1 Corinthians 1:17–18 AMP)

Weakness of God Is Stronger than Men

For it is written: "I will destroy the wisdom of the wise, and bring to nothing the understanding of the prudent."...For since, in the wisdom of God, the world through wisdom did not know God, it pleased God through the foolishness of the message preached to save those who believe. For Jews request a sign, and Greeks seek after wisdom; but we preach Christ crucified, to the Jews a stumbling block and to the Greeks foolishness, but to those who are called, both Jews and Greeks, Christ the power of God and the wisdom of God. Because the foolishness of God is wiser than men, and the weakness of God is stronger than men.

(1 Corinthians 1:19, 21–25)

He Made Us Pure and Holy

God has deliberately chosen to use ideas the world considers foolish and of little worth in order to shame those people considered by the world as wise and great. He has chosen a plan despised by the world, counted as nothing at all, and used it to bring down to nothing those the world considers great, so that no one anywhere can ever brag in the presence of God. For it is from God alone that you have your life through Christ Jesus. He showed us God's plan of salvation; he was the one who made us acceptable to God; he made us pure and holy and gave himself to purchase our salvation.

(1 Corinthians 1:27-30 TLB)

In the Power of God

And I, brethren, when I came to you, did not come with excellence of speech or of wisdom declaring to you the testimony of God. For I determined not to know anything among you except Jesus Christ and Him crucified. I was with you in weakness, in fear, and in much trembling. And my speech and my preaching were not with persuasive words of human wisdom, but in demonstration of the Spirit and of power, that your faith should not be in the wisdom of men but in the power of God.

(1 Corinthians 2:1–5)

The Things That God Has Prepared

But as it is written: "Eye has not seen, nor ear heard, nor have entered into the heart of man the things which God has prepared for those who love Him." (1 Corinthians 2:9)

God Has Revealed Them

But God has revealed them to us through His Spirit. For the Spirit searches all things, yes, the deep things of God. (1 Corinthians 2:10)

We Have the Mind of Christ

Now we have received, not the spirit of the world, but the Spirit who is from God, that we might know the things that have been freely given to us by God. These things we also speak, not in words which man's wisdom teaches but which the Holy Spirit teaches, comparing spiritual things with spiritual. But the natural man does not receive the things of the Spirit of God, for they are foolishness to him; nor can he know them, because they are spiritually discerned. But he who is spiritual judges all things, yet he himself is rightly judged by no one. For "who has known the mind of the LORD that he may instruct Him?" But we have the mind of Christ. (1 Corinthians 2:12–16)

God Gives the Increase

Neither he who plants is anything, nor he who waters, but God who gives the increase. (1 Corinthians 3:7)

You Are God's Building

Now he who plants and he who waters are one, and each one will receive his own reward according to his own labor. For we are God's fellow workers; you are God's field, you are God's building.

(1 Corinthians 3:8–9)

God Dwells in You

Do you not know that you are the temple of God and that the Spirit of God dwells in you?

(1 Corinthians 3:16)

You Are Christ's

And you are Christ's, and Christ is God's.

(1 Corinthians 3:23)

Each One's Praise Will Come from God

Therefore judge nothing before the time, until the Lord comes, who will both bring to light the hidden things of darkness and reveal the counsels of the hearts. Then each one's praise will come from God.

(1 Corinthians 4:5)

So be careful not to jump to conclusions before the Lord returns as to whether someone is a good servant or not. When the Lord comes, he will turn on the light so that everyone can see exactly what each one of us is really like, deep down in our hearts. Then everyone will know why we have been doing the Lord's work. At that time God will give to each one whatever praise is coming to him. (1 Corinthians 4:5 TLB)

In Power

For the kingdom of God is not in word but in power.   (1 Corinthians 4:20)

Living by God's Power

The kingdom of God is not just talking; it is living by God's power.   (1 Corinthians 4:20 TLB)

He Has Accepted You

Those who live immoral lives…will have no share in his kingdom.…There was a time when some of you were just like that but now your sins are washed away, and you are set apart for God, and he has accepted you because of what the Lord Jesus Christ and the Spirit of our God have done for you.

(1 Corinthians 6:9–11 TLB)

Raise Us Up

God both raised up the Lord and will also raise us up by His power.   (1 Corinthians 6:14)

One Spirit with Him

But he who is joined to the Lord is one spirit with Him.   (1 Corinthians 6:17)

Your Body Is the Temple of the Holy Spirit

Do you not know that your body is the temple (the very sanctuary) of the Holy Spirit Who lives within you, Whom you have received [as a Gift] from God? You are not your own, you were bought with a price [purchased with a preciousness and paid for, made His own]. So then, honor God and bring glory to Him in your body. (1 Corinthians 6:19–20 AMP)

Sanctified

The unbelieving husband is sanctified by the wife, and the unbelieving wife is sanctified by the husband. (1 Corinthians 7:14)

Christ's Slave

Let each one remain in the same calling in which he was called. Were you called while a slave? Do not be concerned about it; but if you can be made free, rather use it. For he who is called in the Lord while a slave is the Lord's freedman. Likewise he who is called while free is Christ's slave. (1 Corinthians 7:20–22)

You Were Bought at a Price

You were bought at a price; do not become slaves of men. Brethren, let each one remain with God in that state in which he was called. (1 Corinthians 7:23–24)

He Is Owned by Him

But if one loves God truly [with affectionate reverence, prompt obedience, and grateful recognition of His blessing], he is known by God [recognized as worthy of His intimacy and love, and he is owned by Him].   (1 Corinthians 8:3 AMP)

There Is Only One God

Yet for us there is [only] one God, the Father, Who is the Source of all things and for Whom we [have life], and one Lord, Jesus Christ, through and by Whom are all things and through and by Whom we [ourselves exist].   (1 Corinthians 8:6 AMP)

Will Make the Way of Escape

No temptation has overtaken you except such as is common to man; but God is faithful, who will not allow you to be tempted beyond what you are able, but with the temptation will also make the way of escape, that you may be able to bear it.   (1 Corinthians 10:13)

Parts of the One Body of Christ

When we ask the Lord's blessing upon our drinking from the cup of wine at the Lord's Table, this means, doesn't it, that all who drink it are sharing together the blessing of Christ's blood? And when we break off pieces of the bread from the loaf to eat there together, this shows that we are sharing together in the benefits of his body. No matter how many of us there are, we all eat from the same loaf, showing that we are all parts of the one body of Christ.   (1 Corinthians 10:16–17 TLB)

Earth Is the Lord's

For the [whole] earth is the Lord's and everything that is in it. (1 Corinthians 10:26 AMP)

You Proclaim the Lord's Death

For I received from the Lord that which I also delivered to you: that the Lord Jesus on the same night in which He was betrayed took bread; and when He had given thanks, He broke it and said, "Take, eat; this is My body which is broken for you; do this in remembrance of Me." In the same manner He also took the cup after supper, saying, "This cup is the new covenant in My blood. This do, as often as you drink it, in remembrance of Me." For as often as you eat this bread and drink this cup, you proclaim the Lord's death till He comes. (1 Corinthians 11:23–26)

Not Ignorant

Now concerning spiritual gifts, brethren, I do not want you to be ignorant. (1 Corinthians 12:1)

Except by the Holy Spirit

No one can say that Jesus is Lord except by the Holy Spirit. (1 Corinthians 12:3)

Promises from 1 Corinthians

The Same and Only Holy Spirit

The Holy Spirit displays God's power through each of us as a means of helping the entire church. To one person the Spirit gives the ability to give wise advice; someone else may be especially good at studying and teaching, and this is his gift from the same Spirit. He gives special faith to another, and to someone else the power to heal the sick. He gives power for doing miracles to some, and to others power to prophesy and preach. He gives someone else the power to know whether evil spirits are speaking through those who claim to be giving God's messages—or whether it is really the Spirit of God who is speaking. Still another person is able to speak in languages he never learned; and others, who do not know the language either, are given power to understand what he is saying. It is the same and only Holy Spirit who gives all these gifts and powers, deciding which each one of us should have.

(1 Corinthians 12:7–11 TLB)

Love Never Fails

Love never fails.
(1 Corinthians 13:8)

Love Goes On Forever

All the special gifts and powers from God will someday come to an end, but love goes on forever.
(1 Corinthians 13:8 TLB)

I Will See Everything Clearly

In the same way, we can see and understand only a little about God now, as if we were peering at his reflection in a poor mirror; but someday we are going to see him in his completeness, face to face. Now all that I know is hazy and blurred, but then I will see everything clearly, just as clearly as God sees into my heart right now.
(1 Corinthians 13:12 TLB)

Greatest Is Love

And now abide faith, hope, love, these three; but the greatest of these is love.   (1 Corinthians 13:13)

For Those Who Believe

Therefore tongues are for a sign, not to those who believe but to unbelievers; but prophesying is not for unbelievers but for those who believe.   (1 Corinthians 14:22)

Be Made Alive

For just as [because of their union of nature] in Adam all people die, so also [by virtue of their union of nature] shall all in Christ be made alive.   (1 Corinthians 15:22 AMP)

Will Be Utterly Supreme

After that the end will come when he will turn the kingdom over to God the Father, having put down all enemies of every kind. For Christ will be King until he has defeated all his enemies, including the last enemy—death. This too must be defeated and ended. For the rule and authority over all things has been given to Christ by his Father; except, of course, Christ does not rule over the Father himself, who gave him this power to rule. When Christ has finally won the battle against all his enemies, then he, the Son of God, will put himself also under his Father's orders, so that God who has given him the victory over everything else will be utterly supreme.   (1 Corinthians 15:24–28 TLB)

Raised in Honor and Glory

The sun is glorious in one way, and the moon is glorious in another way, and the stars are glorious in their own [distinctive] way; for one star differs from and surpasses another in its beauty and brilliance. So it is with the resurrection of the dead. [The body] that is sown is perishable and decays, but [the body] that is resurrected is imperishable (immune to decay, immortal). It is sown in dishonor and humiliation; it is raised in honor and glory. It is sown in infirmity and weakness; it is resurrected in strength and endued with power. It is sown a natural (physical) body; it is raised a supernatural (a spiritual) body. [As surely as] there is a physical body, there is also a spiritual body.

(1 Corinthians 15:41–44 AMP)

We Shall Be Given New Bodies

We shall not all die, but we shall all be given new bodies! (1 Corinthians 15:51 TLB)

Death Is Swallowed Up in Victory

When this happens, then at last this Scripture will come true—"Death is swallowed up in victory."

(1 Corinthians 15:54 TLB)

Your Labor Is Not in Vain

Therefore, my beloved brethren, be steadfast, immovable, always abounding in the work of the Lord, knowing that your labor is not in vain in the Lord. (1 Corinthians 15:58)

Promises from 2 Corinthians

Are Comforted by God

Blessed be the God and Father of our Lord Jesus Christ, the Father of mercies and God of all comfort, who comforts us in all our tribulation, that we may be able to comfort those who are in any trouble, with the comfort with which we ourselves are comforted by God.   (2 Corinthians 1:3–4)

Yes and Amen

For all the promises of God in Him are Yes, and in Him Amen, to the glory of God through us.   (2 Corinthians 1:20)

Spirit as a Deposit

Now He who establishes us with you in Christ and has anointed us is God, who also has sealed us and given us the Spirit in our hearts as a guarantee.   (2 Corinthians 1:21)

The Fragrance of Christ

Now thanks be to God who always leads us in triumph in Christ, and through us diffuses the fragrance of His knowledge in every place. For we are to God the fragrance of Christ among those who are being saved and among those who are perishing.   (2 Corinthians 2:14–15)

Carved in Human Hearts

They can see that you are a letter from Christ, written by us. It is not a letter written with pen and ink, but by the Spirit of the living God; not one carved on stone, but in human hearts.

(2 Corinthians 3:3 TLB)

We Are Being Transformed

Now the Lord is the Spirit; and where the Spirit of the Lord is, there is liberty. But we all, with unveiled face, beholding as in a mirror the glory of the Lord, are being transformed into the same image from glory to glory, just as by the Spirit of the Lord.

(2 Corinthians 3:17–18)

Must Be from God

For God, who said, "Let there be light in the darkness," has made us understand that it is the brightness of his glory that is seen in the face of Jesus Christ. But this precious treasure—this light and power that now shine within us—is held in a perishable container, that is, in our weak bodies. Everyone can see that the glorious power within must be from God and is not our own.

(2 Corinthians 4:6 TLB)

Things Not Seen Are Eternal

We do not look at the things which are seen, but at the things which are not seen. For the things which are seen are temporary, but the things which are not seen are eternal.

(2 Corinthians 4:18)

Walk by Faith

For we walk by faith, not by sight.

(2 Corinthians 5:7)

For we walk by faith [we regulate our lives and conduct ourselves by our conviction or belief respecting man's relationship to God and divine things, with trust and holy fervor; thus we walk] not by sight or appearance.

(2 Corinthians 5:7 AMP)

All Things Have Become New

Therefore, if anyone is in Christ, he is a new creation; old things have passed away; behold, all things have become new.

(2 Corinthians 5:17)

He Poured God's Goodness into Us

For God was in Christ, restoring the world to himself, no longer counting men's sins against them but blotting them out. This is the wonderful message he has given us to tell others. We are Christ's ambassadors. God is using us to speak to you: we beg you, as though Christ himself were here pleading with you, receive the love he offers you—be reconciled to God. For God took the sinless Christ and poured into him our sins. Then, in exchange, he poured God's goodness into us.

(2 Corinthians 5:19–21 TLB)

Become the Righteousness of God in Him

Now then, we are ambassadors for Christ, as though God were pleading through us: we implore you on Christ's behalf, be reconciled to God. For He made Him who knew no sin to be sin for us, that we might become the righteousness of God in Him.

(2 Corinthians 5:20–21)

Now Is the Day of Salvation

Behold, now is the accepted time; behold, now is the day of salvation.

(2 Corinthians 6:2)

You Shall Be My Sons and Daughters

You are the temple of the living God. As God has said: "I will dwell in them and walk among them. I will be their God, and they shall be My people." Therefore "Come out from among them and be separate, says the Lord. Do not touch what is unclean, and I will receive you." "I will be a Father to you, and you shall be My sons and daughters, says the LORD Almighty." (2 Corinthians 6:16–18)

Godly Sorrow Produces Repentance

For godly sorrow produces repentance leading to salvation, not to be regretted; but the sorrow of the world produces death. (2 Corinthians 7:10)

You Might Become Rich

For you know the grace of our Lord Jesus Christ, that though He was rich, yet for your sakes He became poor, that you through His poverty might become rich. (2 Corinthians 8:9)

You Have an Abundance

But this I say: He who sows sparingly will also reap sparingly, and he who sows bountifully will also reap bountifully. So let each one give as he purposes in his heart, not grudgingly or of necessity; for God loves a cheerful giver. And God is able to make all grace abound toward you, that you, always having all sufficiency in all things, may have an abundance for every good work.

(2 Corinthians 9:6–8)

But remember this—if you give little, you will get little. A farmer who plants just a few seeds will get only a small crop, but if he plants much, he will reap much. Every one must make up his own mind as to how much he should give. Don't force anyone to give more than he really wants to, for cheerful givers are the ones God prizes. God is able to make it up to you by giving you everything you need and more, so that there will not only be enough for your own needs, but plenty left over to give joyfully to others. (2 Corinthians 9:6–8 TLB)

Grace Is Sufficient

And He said to me, "My grace is sufficient for you, for My strength is made perfect in weakness." Therefore most gladly I will rather boast in my infirmities, that the power of Christ may rest upon me. (2 Corinthians 12:9)

Promises from Daniel

Skill in All Learning and Wisdom

God gave them knowledge and skill in all learning and wisdom and Daniel had understanding in all [kinds of] visions and dreams. (Daniel 1:17 AMP)

He Reveals Deep and Secret Things

Blessed be the name of God forever and ever, for wisdom and might are His. And He changes the times and the seasons; He removes kings and raises up kings; He gives wisdom to the wise and knowledge to those who have understanding. He reveals deep and secret things; He knows what is in the darkness, and light dwells with Him. (Daniel 2:20–22)

God's Kingdom Shall Stand Forever

And in the days of these kings the God of heaven will set up a kingdom which shall never be destroyed; and the kingdom shall not be left to other people; it shall break in pieces and consume all these kingdoms, and it shall stand forever. (Daniel 2:44)

He Will Deliver

Our God whom we serve is able to deliver us from the burning fiery furnace, and He will deliver us from your hand, O king. (Daniel 3:17)

An Everlasting Kingdom

I thought it good to declare the signs and wonders that the Most High God has worked for me. How great are His signs, and how mighty His wonders! His kingdom is an everlasting kingdom, and His dominion is from generation to generation. (Daniel 4:2–3)

Gives It to Whomever He Will

In order that the living may know that the Most High rules in the kingdom of men, gives it to whomever He will. (Daniel 4:17)

Whomever He Chooses

The Most High rules in the kingdom of men, and gives it to whomever He chooses. (Daniel 4:25)

Works Are Truth

Now I, Nebuchadnezzar, praise and extol and honor the King of heaven, all of whose works are truth, and His ways justice. And those who walk in pride He is able to put down. (Daniel 4:37)

Holds Your Breath in His Hand

God…holds your breath in His hand and owns all your ways. (Daniel 5:23)

He Will Deliver You

Your God, whom you serve continually, He will deliver you. (Daniel 6:16)

Because He Believed in His God

"Has your God, whom you serve continually, been able to deliver you from the lions?" Then Daniel said to the king, "O king, live forever! My God sent His angel and shut the lions' mouths, so that they have not hurt me, because I was found innocent before Him; and also, O king, I have done no wrong before you." Then the king was exceedingly glad for him, and commanded that they should take Daniel up out of the den. So Daniel was taken up out of the den, and no injury whatever was found on him, because he believed in his God. (Daniel 6:20–23)

He Works Signs and Wonders

Then King Darius wrote: To all peoples, nations, and languages that dwell in all the earth: Peace be multiplied to you. I make a decree that in every dominion of my kingdom men must tremble and fear before the God of Daniel. For He is the living God, and steadfast forever; His kingdom is the one which shall not be destroyed, and His dominion shall endure to the end. He delivers and rescues, and He works signs and wonders in heaven and on earth, who has delivered Daniel from the power of the lions. (Daniel 6:25–27)

His Kingdom Shall Not Be Destroyed

I saw in the night visions, and behold, on the clouds of the heavens came One like a Son of man, and He came to the Ancient of Days and was presented before Him. And there was given Him [the Messiah] dominion and glory and kingdom, that all peoples, nations, and languages should serve Him. His dominion is an everlasting dominion which shall not pass away, and His kingdom is one which shall not be destroyed. (Daniel 7:13–14 AMP)

Even Forever and Ever

But the saints of the Most High [God] shall receive the kingdom and possess the kingdom forever, even forever and ever. (Daniel 7:18 AMP)

All Dominions Shall Obey Him

Then the kingdom and dominion, and the greatness of the kingdoms under the whole heaven, shall be given to the people, the saints of the Most High. His kingdom is an everlasting kingdom, and all dominions shall serve and obey Him. (Daniel 7:27)

I Have Come because of Your Words

Then he said to me, "Do not fear, Daniel, for from the first day that you set your heart to understand, and to humble yourself before your God, your words were heard; and I have come because of your words." (Daniel 10:12)

Like the Stars Forever and Ever

But at that time your people shall be delivered, everyone whose name shall be found written in the Book [of God's plan for His own]. And many of those who sleep in the dust of the earth shall awake: some to everlasting life and some to shame and everlasting contempt and abhorrence. And the teachers and those who are wise shall shine like the brightness of the firmament, and those who turn many to righteousness (to uprightness and right standing with God) [shall give forth light] like the stars forever and ever. (Daniel 12:1–3 AMP)

Promises from Deuteronomy

You Will Find Him

But from there you will seek the LORD your God, and you will find Him if you seek Him with all your heart and with all your soul. (Deuteronomy 4:29)

There Is None Other

The LORD Himself is God; there is none other besides Him. (Deuteronomy 4:35)

You May Prolong Your Days

Therefore know this day, and consider it in your heart, that the LORD Himself is God in heaven above and on the earth beneath; there is no other. You shall therefore keep His statutes and His commandments which I command you today, that it may go well with you and with your children after you, and that you may prolong your days in the land which the LORD your God is giving you for all time. (Deuteronomy 4:39–40)

That It May Be Well with You

Therefore you shall be careful to do as the LORD your God has commanded you; you shall not turn aside to the right hand or to the left. You shall walk in all the ways which the LORD your God has commanded you, that you may live and that it may be well with you, and that you may prolong your days in the land which you shall possess. (Deuteronomy 5:32–33)

A Special Treasure

For you are a holy people to the LORD your God; the LORD your God has chosen you to be a people for Himself, a special treasure above all the peoples on the face of the earth. (Deuteronomy 7:6)

The Faithful God

Therefore know that the LORD your God, He is God, the faithful God who keeps covenant and mercy for a thousand generations with those who love Him and keep His commandments. (Deuteronomy 7:9)

He Will Love You

And He will love you and bless you and multiply you; He will also bless the fruit of your womb and the fruit of your land, your grain and your new wine and your oil, the increase of your cattle and the offspring of your flock, in the land of which He swore to your fathers to give you.

(Deuteronomy 7:13)

Take Away All Sickness

You shall be blessed above all peoples; there shall not be a male or female barren among you or among your livestock. And the LORD will take away from you all sickness, and will afflict you with none of the terrible diseases of Egypt which you have known, but will lay them on all those who hate you. (Deuteronomy 7:14–15)

Power to Get Wealth

And you shall remember the LORD your God, for it is He who gives you power to get wealth, that He may establish His covenant which He swore to your fathers, as it is this day.　　(Deuteronomy 8:18)

Because the Lord Your God Loves You

Nevertheless the LORD your God would not listen to Balaam, but the LORD your God turned the curse into a blessing for you, because the LORD your God loves you.　　(Deuteronomy 23:5)

Peculiar People

And the Lord has declared this day that you are His peculiar people as He promised you, and you are to keep all His commandments; and He will make you high above all nations which He has made, in praise and in fame and in honor, and that you shall be a holy people to the Lord your God, as He has spoken.

(Deuteronomy 26:18–19 AMP)

The Lord Shall Make You the Head

If you will listen diligently to the voice of the Lord your God, being watchful to do all His commandments which I command you this day, the Lord your God will set you high above all the nations of the earth. And all these blessings shall come upon you and overtake you if you heed the voice of the Lord your God. Blessed shall you be in the city and blessed shall you be in the field. Blessed shall be the fruit of your body and the fruit of your ground and the fruit of your beasts, the increase of your cattle and the young of your flock. Blessed shall be your basket and your kneading trough. Blessed shall you be when you come in and blessed shall you be when you go out. The Lord shall cause your enemies who rise up against you to be defeated before your face; they shall come out against you one way and flee before you seven ways. The Lord shall command the blessing upon you in your storehouse and in all that you undertake. And He will bless you in the land which the Lord your God gives you. The Lord will establish you as a people holy to Himself, as He has sworn to you, if you keep the commandments of the Lord your God and walk in His ways. And all people of the earth shall see that you are called by the name [and in the presence of] the Lord, and they shall be afraid of you. And the Lord shall make you have a surplus of prosperity, through the fruit of your body, of your livestock, and of your ground, in the land which the Lord swore to your fathers to give you. The Lord shall open to you His good treasury, the heavens, to give the rain of your land in its season and to bless all the work of your hands; and you shall lend to many nations, but you shall not borrow. And the Lord shall make you the head, and not the tail; and you shall be above only, and you shall not be beneath, if you heed the commandments of the Lord your God which I command you this day and are watchful to do them.

(Deuteronomy 28:1–13 AMP)

Make You Abundantly Prosperous

And the Lord your God will make you abundantly prosperous in every work of your hand, in the fruit of your body, of your cattle, of your land, for good; for the Lord will again delight in prospering you, as He took delight in your fathers, if you obey the voice of the Lord your God, to keep His commandments and His statutes which are written in this Book of the Law, and if you turn to the Lord your God with all your [mind and] heart and with all your being. (Deuteronomy 30:9–10 AMP)

Choose Life

I call heaven and earth as witnesses today against you, that I have set before you life and death, blessing and cursing; therefore choose life, that both you and your descendants may live.

(Deuteronomy 30:19)

He Will Not Leave You

Be strong and of good courage, do not fear nor be afraid of them; for the LORD your God, He is the One who goes with you. He will not leave you nor forsake you.   (Deuteronomy 31:6)

Not Leave or Forsake You

And the LORD, He is the one who goes before you. He will be with you, He will not leave you nor forsake you; do not fear nor be dismayed.   (Deuteronomy 31:8)

Righteous and Upright

He is the Rock, His work is perfect; for all His ways are justice, a God of truth and without injustice; righteous and upright is He.   (Deuteronomy 32:4)

God Is Your Refuge

The eternal God is your refuge, and underneath are the everlasting arms; He will thrust out the enemy from before you, and will say, "Destroy!"   (Deuteronomy 33:27)

Promises from Ecclesiastes

The Earth Abides Forever

One generation passes away, and another generation comes; but the earth abides forever.
                                                                (Ecclesiastes 1:4)

They Return Again

The sun also rises, and the sun goes down, and hastens to the place where it arose. The wind goes toward the south, and turns around to the north; the wind whirls about continually, and comes again on its circuit. All the rivers run into the sea, yet the sea is not full; to the place from which the rivers come, there they return again.   (Ecclesiastes 1:5–7)

There Is Nothing New

That which has been is what will be, that which is done is what will be done, and there is nothing new under the sun. Is there anything of which it may be said, "See, this is new"? It has already been in ancient times before us. There is no remembrance of former things, nor will there be any remembrance of things that are to come by those who will come after.   (Ecclesiastes 1:9–11)

To Him Who Is Good before God

For God gives wisdom and knowledge and joy to a man who is good in His sight; but to the sinner He gives the work of gathering and collecting, that he may give to him who is good before God.

(Ecclesiastes 2:26)

A Time for Every Purpose

To everything there is a season, a time for every purpose under heaven: a time to be born, and a time to die; a time to plant, and a time to pluck what is planted; a time to kill, and a time to heal; a time to break down, and a time to build up; a time to weep, and a time to laugh; a time to mourn, and a time to dance; a time to cast away stones, and a time to gather stones; a time to embrace, and a time to refrain from embracing; a time to gain, and a time to lose; a time to keep, and a time to throw away; a time to tear, and a time to sew; a time to keep silence, and a time to speak; a time to love, and a time to hate; a time of war, and a time of peace.

(Ecclesiastes 3:1–8)

He Has Put Eternity in Their Hearts

He has made everything beautiful in its time. Also He has put eternity in their hearts.

(Ecclesiastes 3:11)

It Shall Be Forever

Whatever God does, it shall be forever. Nothing can be added to it, and nothing taken from it. God does it, that men should fear before Him. That which is has already been, and what is to be has already been; and God requires an account of what is past.

(Ecclesiastes 3:14–15)

Promises from Ecclesiastes

A Threefold Cord Is Not Quickly Broken

Two are better than one, because they have a good reward for their labor. For if they fall, one will lift up his companion. But woe to him who is alone when he falls, for he has no one to help him up. Again, if two lie down together, they will keep warm; but how can one be warm alone? Though one may be overpowered by another, two can withstand him. And a threefold cord is not quickly broken.

(Ecclesiastes 4:9–12)

Do Not Delay

When you make a vow to God, do not delay to pay it; for He has no pleasure in fools. Pay what you have vowed; better not to vow than to vow and not pay.

(Ecclesiastes 5:4–5)

The Joy of His Heart

As for every man to whom God has given riches and wealth, and given him power to eat of it, to receive his heritage and rejoice in his labor; this is the gift of God. For he will not dwell unduly on the days of his life, because God keeps him busy with the joy of his heart.

(Ecclesiastes 5:19–20)

A Good Name

A good name is better than precious ointment.

(Ecclesiastes 7:1)

Wisdom Gives Life

Wisdom is good with an inheritance, and profitable to those who see the sun. For wisdom is a defense as money is a defense, but the excellence of knowledge is that wisdom gives life to those who have it.

(Ecclesiastes 7:11–12)

He Who Fears God

Do not be overly righteous, nor be overly wise: why should you destroy yourself? Do not be overly wicked, nor be foolish: why should you die before your time? It is good that you grasp this, and also not remove your hand from the other; for he who fears God will escape them all.

(Ecclesiastes 7:16–18)

His Face Shines

A man's wisdom makes his face shine.

(Ecclesiastes 8:1)

A Man Has Nothing Better

A man has nothing better under the sun than to eat, drink, and be merry; for this will remain with him in his labor for the days of his life which God gives him under the sun.

(Ecclesiastes 8:15)

Do It with Your Might

Whatever your hand finds to do, do it with your might.

(Ecclesiastes 9:10)

Better than Strength

Wisdom is better than strength.

(Ecclesiastes 9:16)

Better than Weapons

Wisdom is better than weapons of war.

(Ecclesiastes 9:18)

Success

Wisdom brings success. (Ecclesiastes 10:10)

You Will Find It

Cast your bread upon the waters, for you will find it after many days. (Ecclesiastes 11:1)

Promises from Ephesians

He Has Made Us Accepted

Blessed be the God and Father of our Lord Jesus Christ, who has blessed us with every spiritual blessing in the heavenly places in Christ, just as He chose us in Him before the foundation of the world, that we should be holy and without blame before Him in love, having predestined us to adoption as sons by Jesus Christ to Himself, according to the good pleasure of His will, to the praise of the glory of His grace, by which He has made us accepted in the Beloved. (Ephesians 1:3–6)

Redemption

In Him we have redemption through His blood, the forgiveness of sins, according to the riches of His grace. (Ephesians 1:7)

To Be with Him in Christ Forever

God has told us his secret reason for sending Christ, a plan he decided on in mercy long ago; and this was his purpose: that when the time is ripe he will gather us all together from wherever we are—in heaven or on earth—to be with him in Christ, forever. (Ephesians 1:9–10 TLB)

Marked as Belonging to Christ

And because of what Christ did, all you others too, who heard the Good News about how to be saved, and trusted Christ, were marked as belonging to Christ by the Holy Spirit, who long ago had been promised to all of us Christians. (Ephesians 1:13 TLB)

He Guarantees to Bring Us to Himself

His presence within us is God's guarantee that he really will give us all that he promised; and the Spirit's seal upon us means that God has already purchased us and that he guarantees to bring us to himself. This is just one more reason for us to praise our glorious God. (Ephesians 1:14 TLB)

God Has Been Made Rich

I pray that your hearts will be flooded with light so that you can see something of the future he has called you to share. I want you to realize that God has been made rich because we who are Christ's have been given to him! (Ephesians 1:18 TLB)

In This World or in the World to Come

I pray that you will begin to understand how incredibly great his power is to help those who believe him. It is that same mighty power that raised Christ from the dead and seated him in the place of honor at God's right hand in heaven, far, far above any other king or ruler or dictator or leader. Yes, his honor is far more glorious than that of anyone else either in this world or in the world to come.

(Ephesians 1:19–21 TLB)

The Author and Giver of Everything

And God has put all things under his feet and made him the supreme Head of the church—which is his body, filled with himself, the Author and Giver of everything everywhere.   (Ephesians 1:22–23 TLB)

You He Made Alive

And you He made alive, who were dead in trespasses and sins, in which you once walked according to the course of this world, according to the prince of the power of the air, the spirit who now works in the sons of disobedience.   (Ephesians 2:1–2)

Sit with Him in the Heavenly Realms

All of us used to be just as they are, our lives expressing the evil within us, doing every wicked thing that our passions or our evil thoughts might lead us into. We started out bad, being born with evil natures, and were under God's anger just like everyone else. But God is so rich in mercy; he loved us so much that even though we were spiritually dead and doomed by our sins, he gave us back our lives again when he raised Christ from the dead—only by his undeserved favor have we ever been saved—and lifted us up from the grave into glory along with Christ, where we sit with him in the heavenly realms—all because of what Christ Jesus did.   (Ephesians 2:3–6 TLB)

Trusting Is a Gift from God

And now God can always point to us as examples of how very, very rich his kindness is, as shown in all he has done for us through Jesus Christ. Because of his kindness, you have been saved through trusting Christ. And even trusting is not of yourselves; it too is a gift from God.

(Ephesians 2:7–8 TLB)

Given Us New Lives from Christ Jesus

It is God himself who has made us what we are and given us new lives from Christ Jesus; and long ages ago he planned that we should spend these lives in helping others. (Ephesians 2:10 TLB)

With His Blood

But now you belong to Christ Jesus, and though you once were far away from God, now you have been brought very near to him because of what Jesus Christ has done for you with his blood.

(Ephesians 2:13 TLB)

Way of Peace

For Christ himself is our way of peace. He has made peace between us Jews and you Gentiles by making us all one family, breaking down the wall of contempt that used to separate us. (Ephesians 2:14 TLB)

Part of This Dwelling Place of God

Now you are no longer strangers to God and foreigners to heaven, but you are members of God's very own family, citizens of God's country, and you belong in God's household with every other Christian. What a foundation you stand on now: the apostles and the prophets; and the cornerstone of the building is Jesus Christ himself! We who believe are carefully joined together with Christ as parts of a beautiful, constantly growing temple for God. And you also are joined with him and with each other by the Spirit and are part of this dwelling place of God.   (Ephesians 2:19–22 TLB)

Endless Treasures

Just think! Though I did nothing to deserve it, and though I am the most useless Christian there is, yet I was the one chosen for this special joy of telling the Gentiles the Glad News of the endless treasures available to them in Christ; and to explain to everyone that God is the Savior of the Gentiles too, just as he who made all things had secretly planned from the very beginning.   (Ephesians 3:8–9 TLB)

We Can Come Fearlessly

Now we can come fearlessly right into God's presence, assured of his glad welcome when we come with Christ and trust in him.   (Ephesians 3:12 TLB)

His Plan

When I think of the wisdom and scope of his plan I fall down on my knees and pray to the Father of all the great family of God—some of them already in heaven and some down here on earth.

(Ephesians 3:14 TLB)

Living within You

And I pray that Christ will be more and more at home in your hearts, living within you as you trust in him.   (Ephesians 3:17 TLB)

You Will Be Filled Up with God Himself

May your roots go down deep into the soil of God's marvelous love; and may you be able to feel and understand, as all God's children should, how long, how wide, how deep, and how high his love really is; and to experience this love for yourselves, though it is so great that you will never see the end of it or fully know or understand it. And so at last you will be filled up with God himself.   (Ephesians 3:17–19 TLB)

His Mighty Power

Now glory be to God who by his mighty power at work within us is able to do far more than we would ever dare to ask or even dream of—infinitely beyond our highest prayers, desires, thoughts, or hopes.   (Ephesians 3:20 TLB)

One Body

We are all parts of one body, we have the same Spirit, and we have all been called to the same glorious future.   (Ephesians 4:4 TLB)

Only One

For us there is only one Lord, one faith, one baptism.   (Ephesians 4:5 TLB)

Like Christ

Instead, we will lovingly follow the truth at all times—speaking truly, dealing truly, living truly—and so become more and more in every way like Christ who is the Head of his body, the church. Under his direction the whole body is fitted together perfectly, and each part in its own special way helps the other parts, so that the whole body is healthy and growing and full of love. (Ephesians 4:15 TLB)

Sweet Perfume to Him

Follow God's example in everything you do just as a much loved child imitates his father. Be full of love for others, following the example of Christ who loved you and gave himself to God as a sacrifice to take away your sins. And God was pleased, for Christ's love for you was like sweet perfume to him. (Ephesians 5:1–2 TLB)

Full of Light

For though once your heart was full of darkness, now it is full of light from the Lord, and your behavior should show it! (Ephesians 5:8 TLB)

Full of Blessing

And this is the promise: that if you honor your father and mother, yours will be a long life, full of blessing. (Ephesians 6:3 TLB)

The Lord Will Pay You

Remember, the Lord will pay you for each good thing you do, whether you are slave or free. (Ephesians 6:8 TLB)

Quench All the Fiery Darts of the Wicked One

Put on the whole armor of God, that you may be able to stand against the wiles of the devil. For we do not wrestle against flesh and blood, but against principalities, against powers, against the rulers of the darkness of this age, against spiritual hosts of wickedness in the heavenly places. Therefore take up the whole armor of God, that you may be able to withstand in the evil day, and having done all, to stand. Stand therefore, having girded your waist with truth, having put on the breastplate of righteousness, and having shod your feet with the preparation of the gospel of peace; above all, taking the shield of faith with which you will be able to quench all the fiery darts of the wicked one. And take the helmet of salvation, and the sword of the Spirit, which is the word of God.   (Ephesians 6:11–17)

Promises from Esther

Such a Time as This

"You have come to the kingdom for such a time as this?"   (Esther 4:14)

Promises from Exodus

I Am Who I Am

Then Moses said to God, "Indeed, when I come to the children of Israel and say to them, 'The God of your fathers has sent me to you,' and they say to me, 'What is His name?' what shall I say to them?" And God said to Moses, "I AM WHO I AM."   (Exodus 3:13–14)

My Name May Be Declared

But indeed for this purpose I have raised you up, that I may show My power in you, and that My name may be declared in all the earth. (Exodus 9:16)

You Have Guided Them

Who is like You, O LORD, among the gods? Who is like You, glorious in holiness, fearful in praises, doing wonders? You stretched out Your right hand; the earth swallowed them. You in Your mercy have led forth the people whom You have redeemed; You have guided them in Your strength to Your holy habitation. (Exodus 15:11–13)

I Am the Lord Who Heals You

If you diligently heed the voice of the LORD your God and do what is right in His sight, give ear to His commandments and keep all His statutes, I will put none of the diseases on you which I have brought on the Egyptians. For I am the LORD who heals you. (Exodus 15:26)

A Special Treasure to Me

Now therefore, if you will indeed obey My voice and keep My covenant, then you shall be a special treasure to Me above all people; for all the earth is Mine. (Exodus 19:5)

Bless Your Bread and Your Water

So you shall serve the LORD your God, and He will bless your bread and your water. And I will take sickness away from the midst of you. No one shall suffer miscarriage or be barren in your land; I will fulfill the number of your days. (Exodus 23:25–26)

I Make a Covenant

And He said: "Behold, I make a covenant. Before all your people I will do marvels such as have not been done in all the earth, nor in any nation; and all the people among whom you are shall see the work of the LORD. For it is an awesome thing that I will do with you." (Exodus 34:10)

Promises from Ezekiel

The Glory of the Lord

And above the firmament that was over their heads was the likeness of a throne in appearance like a sapphire stone, and seated above the likeness of a throne was a likeness with the appearance of a Man. From what had the appearance of His waist upward, I saw a lustre as it were glowing metal with the appearance of fire enclosed round about within it; and from the appearance of His waist downward, I saw as it were the appearance of fire, and there was brightness [of a halo] round about Him. Like the appearance of the bow that is in the cloud on the day of rain, so was the appearance of the brightness round about. This was the appearance of the likeness of the glory of the Lord. And when I saw it, I fell upon my face and I heard a voice of One speaking. (Ezekiel 1:26–28 AMP)

Like Honey in Sweetness

Moreover He said to me, "Son of man, eat what you find; eat this scroll, and go, speak to the house of Israel." So I opened my mouth, and He caused me to eat that scroll. And He said to me, "Son of man, feed your belly, and fill your stomach with this scroll that I give you." So I ate, and it was in my mouth like honey in sweetness. (Ezekiel 3:1–3)

Blessed Is the Glory

I heard behind me a great thunderous voice: "Blessed is the glory of the LORD from His place!"
(Ezekiel 3:12)

Delivered from Guilt

Nevertheless if you warn the righteous man not to sin, and he does not sin, he shall surely live because he is warned; also you have delivered yourself from guilt.   (Ezekiel 3:21 AMP)

I Will Be Their God

Then I will give them one heart, and I will put a new spirit within them, and take the stony heart out of their flesh, and give them a heart of flesh, that they may walk in My statutes and keep My judgments and do them; and they shall be My people, and I will be their God.   (Ezekiel 11:19–20)

Everlasting Covenant

Nevertheless I will remember My covenant with you in the days of your youth, and I will establish an everlasting covenant with you.   (Ezekiel 16:60)

I Am the Lord

And I will establish My covenant with you. Then you shall know that I am the LORD.
(Ezekiel 16:62)

He Shall Surely Live

"If he has walked in My statutes and kept My judgments faithfully; He is just; He shall surely live!" says the Lord GOD.   (Ezekiel 18:9)

He Shall Not Die

Again, when a wicked man turns away from the wickedness which he committed, and does what is lawful and right, he preserves himself alive. Because he considers and turns away from all the transgressions which he committed, he shall surely live; he shall not die.   (Ezekiel 18:27–28)

I Seek Out My Sheep

For thus says the Lord GOD: "Indeed I Myself will search for My sheep and seek them out. As a shepherd seeks out his flock on the day he is among his scattered sheep, so will I seek out My sheep and deliver them from all the places where they were scattered on a cloudy and dark day."
                                                                                           (Ezekiel 34:11–12)

Bring Back What Was Broken

"I will feed My flock, and I will make them lie down," says the Lord GOD. "I will seek what was lost and bring back what was driven away, bind up the broken and strengthen what was sick."
                                                                                           (Ezekiel 34:15–16)

Give You a New Heart

I will give you a new heart and put a new spirit within you; I will take the heart of stone out of your flesh and give you a heart of flesh.   (Ezekiel 36:26)

Promises from Ezekiel

The Sovereign Ruler

Thus will I demonstrate My greatness and My holiness, and I will be recognized, understood, and known in the eyes of many nations; yes, they shall know that I am the Lord [the Sovereign Ruler, Who calls forth loyalty and obedient service].   (Ezekiel 38:23 AMP)

I Am the Lord Their God

And I will manifest My honor and glory among the nations, and all the nations shall see My judgment and justice [in the punishment] which I have executed and My hand which I have laid on them. So the house of Israel shall know, understand, and realize beyond all question that I am the Lord their God from that day forward.   (Ezekiel 39:21–22 AMP)

Blessing on Your House

The best of all firstfruits of any kind, and every sacrifice of any kind from all your sacrifices, shall be the priest's; also you shall give to the priest the first of your ground meal, to cause a blessing to rest on your house.   (Ezekiel 44:30)

Name of the City

And the name of the city from that day shall be: THE LORD IS THERE.   (Ezekiel 48:35)

Promises from Ezra

Mercy Endures Forever

For He is good, for His mercy endures forever toward Israel. (Ezra 3:11)

God's Hand on Those Who Seek Him

The hand of our God is upon all those for good who seek Him, but His power and His wrath are against all those who forsake Him. (Ezra 8:22)

Promises from Galatians

Rescued Us from This Evil World

May peace and blessing be yours from God the Father and from the Lord Jesus Christ. He died for our sins just as God our Father planned, and rescued us from this evil world in which we live. (Galatians 1:3–4 TLB)

I Have Been Crucified

I have been crucified with Christ: and I myself no longer live, but Christ lives in me. And the real life I now have within this body is a result of my trusting in the Son of God, who loved me and gave himself for me. (Galatians 2:20 TLB)

Christ Lives in Me

I have been crucified with Christ; it is no longer I who live, but Christ lives in me; and the life which I now live in the flesh I live by faith in the Son of God, who loved me and gave Himself for me. (Galatians 2:20)

Same Blessing

All who trust in Christ share the same blessing Abraham received. (Galatians 3:9 TLB)

By Faith

But that no one is justified by the law in the sight of God is evident, for "the just shall live by faith." (Galatians 3:11)

Redeemed from the Curse

Christ has redeemed us from the curse of the law, having become a curse for us (for it is written, "Cursed is everyone who hangs on a tree"), that the blessing of Abraham might come upon the Gentiles in Christ Jesus, that we might receive the promise of the Spirit through faith. (Galatians 3:13–14)

We Are Enveloped by Him

For now we are all children of God through faith in Jesus Christ, and we who have been baptized into union with Christ are enveloped by him.   (Galatians 3:26–27 TLB)

We Are One

We are no longer Jews or Greeks or slaves or free men or even merely men or women, but we are all the same—we are Christians; we are one in Christ Jesus.   (Galatians 3:28 TLB)

God's Promises to Him Belong to Us

And now that we are Christ's we are the true descendants of Abraham, and all of God's promises to him belong to us.   (Galatians 3:29 TLB)

Everything He Has Belongs to Us

And because we are his sons God has sent the Spirit of his Son into our hearts, so now we can rightly speak of God as our dear Father. Now we are no longer slaves, but God's own sons. And since we are his sons, everything he has belongs to us, for that is the way God planned.   (Galatians 4:6–7 TLB)

We Will Reap a Harvest of Blessing

If he plants the good things of the Spirit, he will reap the everlasting life which the Holy Spirit gives him. And let us not get tired of doing what is right, for after a while we will reap a harvest of blessing if we don't get discouraged and give up.   (Galatians 6:8–9 TLB)

It Was Excellent in Every Way

When God began creating the heavens and the earth, the earth was at first a shapeless, chaotic mass, with the Spirit of God brooding over the dark vapors. Then God said, "Let there be light." And light appeared. And God was pleased with it, and divided the light from the darkness. So he let it shine for awhile, and then there was darkness again. He called the light "daytime," and the darkness "night-time." Together they formed the first day. And God said, "Let the vapors separate to form the sky above and the oceans below." So God made the sky, dividing the vapor above from the water below. This all happened on the second day. Then God said, "Let the water beneath the sky be gathered into oceans so that the dry land will emerge." And so it was. Then God named the dry land "earth," and the water "seas." And God was pleased. And he said, "Let the earth burst forth with every sort of grass and seed-bearing plant, and fruit trees with seeds inside the fruit, so that these seeds will produce the kinds of plants and fruits they came from." And so it was, and God was pleased. This all occurred on the third day. Then God said, "Let there be bright lights in the sky to give light to the earth and to identify the day and the night; they shall bring about the seasons on the earth, and mark the days and years." And so it was. For God made two huge lights, the sun and moon, to shine down upon the earth—the larger one, the sun, to preside over the day and the smaller one, the moon, to preside through the night; he also made the stars. And God set them in the sky to light the earth, and to preside over the day and night, and to divide the light from the darkness. And God was pleased. This all happened on the fourth day. Then God said, "Let the waters teem with fish and other life, and let the skies be filled with birds of every kind." So God created great sea creatures, and every sort of fish and every kind of bird. And God looked at them with pleasure, and blessed them all. "Multiply and stock the oceans," he told them, and to the birds he said, "Let your numbers increase. Fill the earth!" That ended the fifth day. And God said, "Let the earth bring forth every kind of animal—cattle and reptiles and wildlife of every kind." And so it was. God made all sorts of wild animals and cattle and reptiles. And God was pleased with what he had done. Then God said, "Let us make a man—someone like ourselves, to be the master of all life upon the earth and in the skies and in the seas." So God made man like his Maker. Like God did God make man; Man and maid did he make them. And God blessed them and told them, "Multiply and fill the earth and subdue it; you are masters of the fish and birds and all the animals. And look! I have given you the seed-bearing plants throughout the earth and all the fruit trees for your food. And I've given all the grass and plants to the animals and birds for their food." Then God looked over all that he had made, and it was excellent in every way. This ended the sixth day. Now at last the heavens and earth were successfully completed, with all that they contained. So on the seventh day, having finished his task, God ceased from this work he had been doing, and God blessed the seventh day and declared it holy, because it was the day when he ceased this work of creation.

(Genesis 1:1–31; 2:1–3)

They Shall Become One Flesh

And the LORD God said, "It is not good that man should be alone; I will make him a helper comparable to him." Out of the ground the LORD God formed every beast of the field and every bird of the air, and brought them to Adam to see what he would call them. And whatever Adam called each living creature, that was its name. So Adam gave names to all cattle, to the birds of the air, and to every beast of the field. But for Adam there was not found a helper comparable to him. And the LORD God caused a deep sleep to fall on Adam, and he slept; and He took one of his ribs, and closed up the flesh in its place. Then the rib which the LORD God had taken from man He made into a woman, and He brought her to the man. And Adam said: "This is now bone of my bones and flesh of my flesh; she shall be called Woman, because she was taken out of Man." Therefore a man shall leave his father and mother and be joined to his wife, and they shall become one flesh.

(Genesis 2:18–24)

Establish My Covenant

But I will establish My covenant with you.

(Genesis 6:18)

Never Again

And the LORD smelled a soothing aroma. Then the LORD said in His heart, "I will never again curse the ground for man's sake, although the imagination of man's heart is evil from his youth; nor will I again destroy every living thing as I have done." (Genesis 8:21)

Earth Remains

While the earth remains, seedtime and harvest, cold and heat, winter and summer, and day and night shall not cease. (Genesis 8:22)

This Is the Sign of the Covenant

And I seal this promise with this sign: I have placed my rainbow in the clouds as a sign of my promise until the end of time, to you and to all the earth. When I send clouds over the earth, the rainbow will be seen in the clouds, and I will remember my promise to you and to every being, that never again will the floods come and destroy all life. For I will see the rainbow in the cloud and remember my eternal promise to every living being on the earth. (Genesis 9:12–16 TLB)

Earth Shall Be Blessed

I will bless those who bless you, and I will curse him who curses you; and in you all the families of the earth shall be blessed. (Genesis 12:3)

I Am Your Shield

I am your shield, your exceedingly great reward. (Genesis 15:1)

For Righteousness

"Look now toward heaven, and count the stars if you are able to number them." And He said to him, "So shall your descendants be." And he believed in the LORD, and He accounted it to him for righteousness.

(Genesis 15:5–6)

An Everlasting Covenant

When Abram was ninety-nine years old, the LORD appeared to Abram and said to him, "I am Almighty God; walk before Me and be blameless. And I will make My covenant between Me and you, and will multiply you exceedingly." Then Abram fell on his face, and God talked with him, saying: "As for Me, behold, My covenant is with you, and you shall be a father of many nations. No longer shall your name be called Abram, but your name shall be Abraham; for I have made you a father of many nations. I will make you exceedingly fruitful; and I will make nations of you, and kings shall come from you. And I will establish My covenant between Me and you and your descendants after you in their generations, for an everlasting covenant, to be God to you and your descendants after you."

(Genesis 17:1–7)

His Descendants after Him

Then God said: "...Sarah your wife shall bear you a son, and you shall call his name Isaac; I will establish My covenant with him for an everlasting covenant, and with his descendants after him."

(Genesis 17:19)

Nothing Too Hard for the Lord

Is anything too hard for the LORD?

(Genesis 18:14)

Promises from Genesis

All the Nations of the Earth Shall Be Blessed

And Abraham called the name of the place, The-Lord-Will-Provide; as it is said to this day, "In the Mount of The Lord it shall be provided." Then the Angel of the Lord called to Abraham a second time out of heaven, and said: "By Myself I have sworn, says the Lord, because you have done this thing, and have not withheld your son, your only son; blessing I will bless you, and in multiplying I will multiply your descendants as the stars of the heaven and as the sand which is on the seashore; and your descendants shall possess the gate of their enemies. In your seed all the nations of the earth shall be blessed, because you have obeyed My voice." (Genesis 22:14–18)

In Your Seed

And I will make your descendants multiply as the stars of heaven; I will give to your descendants all these lands; and in your seed all the nations of the earth shall be blessed. (Genesis 26:4)

A Hundredfold

Then Isaac sowed in that land, and reaped in the same year a hundredfold; and the Lord blessed him. (Genesis 26:12)

Will Keep You

Then he dreamed, and behold, a ladder was set up on the earth, and its top reached to heaven; and there the angels of God were ascending and descending on it. And behold, the LORD stood above it and said: "I am the LORD God of Abraham your father and the God of Isaac; the land on which you lie I will give to you and your descendants. Also your descendants shall be as the dust of the earth; you shall spread abroad to the west and the east, to the north and the south; and in you and in your seed all the families of the earth shall be blessed. Behold, I am with you and will keep you wherever you go, and will bring you back to this land; for I will not leave you until I have done what I have spoken to you."

(Genesis 28:12–15)

Kings Shall Come from Your Body

I am God Almighty. Be fruitful and multiply; a nation and a company of nations shall proceed from you, and kings shall come from your body.

(Genesis 35:11)

Promises from Habakkuk

Be Utterly Astounded

Look among the nations and watch; be utterly astounded! For I will work a work in your days which you would not believe, though it were told you.

(Habakkuk 1:5)

Look around [you, Habakkuk, replied the Lord] among the nations and see! And be astonished! Astounded! For I am putting into effect a work in your days [such] that you would not believe it if it were told you.

(Habukkuk 1:5 AMP)

It Will Not Tarry

Write the vision and make it plain on tablets, that he may run who reads it. For the vision is yet for an appointed time; but at the end it will speak, and it will not lie. Though it tarries, wait for it; because it will surely come, it will not tarry. (Habukkuk 2:2–3)

It Will Surely Come

And the Lord answered me and said, Write the vision, and engrave it so plainly upon tablets that everyone who passes may [be able to] read [it easily and quickly] as he hastens by. For the vision is yet for an appointed time and it hastens to the end [fulfillment]; it will not deceive or disappoint. Though it tarry, wait [earnestly] for it, because it will surely come; it will not be behindhand on its appointed day. (Habukkuk 2:2–3 AMP)

Live by His Faith

Look at the proud; his soul is not straight or right within him, but the [rigidly] just and the [uncompromisingly] righteous man shall live by his faith and in his faithfulness. (Habukkuk 2:4 AMP)

As the Waters Cover the Sea

For the earth will be filled with the knowledge of the glory of the LORD, as the waters cover the sea. (Habukkuk 2:14)

There His Power Was Hidden

God came from Teman, the Holy One from Mount Paran. Selah His glory covered the heavens, and the earth was full of His praise. His brightness was like the light; He had rays flashing from His hand, and there His power was hidden. (Habukkuk 3:3–4)

His Power Is Just the Same

I see God moving across the deserts from Mount Sinai. His brilliant splendor fills the earth and sky; his glory fills the heavens, and the earth is full of his praise! What a wonderful God he is! From his hands flash rays of brilliant light. He rejoices in his awesome power. Pestilence marches before him; plague follows close behind. He stops; he stands still for a moment, gazing at the earth. Then he shakes the nations, scattering the everlasting mountains and leveling the hills. His power is just the same as always! (Habukkuk 3:3–6 TLB)

He Makes Me Walk on High Hills

Though the fig tree may not blossom, nor fruit be on the vines; though the labor of the olive may fail, and the fields yield no food; though the flock may be cut off from the fold, and there be no herd in the stalls; yet I will rejoice in the LORD, I will joy in the God of my salvation. The LORD God is my strength; He will make my feet like deer's feet, and He will make me walk on my high hills. (Habukkuk 3:17–19)

Spiritual Progress

The Lord God is my Strength, my personal bravery, and my invincible army; He makes my feet like hinds' feet and will make me to walk [not to stand still in terror, but to walk] and make [spiritual] progress upon my high places [of trouble, suffering or responsibility]! (Habukkuk 3:19 AMP)

Promises from Haggai

I Will Give Peace

"For thus says the LORD of hosts: 'Once more (it is a little while) I will shake heaven and earth, the sea and dry land; and I will shake all nations, and they shall come to the Desire of All Nations, and I will fill this temple with glory,' says the LORD of hosts. 'The glory of this latter temple shall be greater than the former,' says the LORD of hosts. 'And in this place I will give peace,' says the LORD of hosts."
(Haggai 2:6–7, 9)

From This Day Forward

Is the seed still in the barn? As yet the vine, the fig tree, the pomegranate, and the olive tree have not yielded fruit. But from this day forward I will bless you.
(Haggai 2:19)

Promises from Hebrews

Far Greater than Names of the Angels

Long ago God spoke in many different ways to our fathers through the prophets [in visions, dreams, and even face to face], telling them little by little about his plans. But now in these days he has spoken to us through his Son to whom he has given everything, and through whom he made the world and everything there is. God's Son shines out with God's glory, and all that God's Son is and does marks him as God. He regulates the universe by the mighty power of his command. He is the one who died to cleanse us and clear our record of all sin, and then sat down in highest honor beside the great God of heaven. Thus he became far greater than the angels, as proved by the fact that his name "Son of God," which was passed on to him from his Father, is far greater than the names and titles of the angels.

(Hebrews 1:1–4 TLB)

Oil of Exultant Joy

Referring to the angels He says, [God] Who makes His angels winds and His ministering servants flames of fire; but as to the Son, He says to Him, Your throne, O God, is forever and ever (to the ages of the ages), and the scepter of Your kingdom is a scepter of absolute righteousness (of justice and straightforwardness). You have loved righteousness [You have delighted in integrity, virtue, and uprightness in purpose, thought, and action] and You have hated lawlessness (injustice and iniquity). Therefore God, [even] Your God (Godhead), has anointed You with the oil of exultant joy and gladness above and beyond Your companions.

(Hebrews 1:7–9 AMP)

God Showed His Approval

How shall we escape [appropriate retribution] if we neglect and refuse to pay attention to such a great salvation [as is now offered to us, letting it drift past us forever]? For it was declared at first by the Lord [Himself], and it was confirmed to us and proved to be real and genuine by those who personally heard [Him speak]. [Besides this evidence] it was also established and plainly endorsed by God, Who showed His approval of it by signs and wonders and various miraculous manifestations of [His] power and by imparting the gifts of the Holy Spirit [to the believers] according to His own will. (Hebrews 2:3–4 AMP)

All Things under His Feet

What is man that You are mindful of him, or the son of man that You take care of him? You have made him a little lower than the angels; You have crowned him with glory and honor, and set him over the works of Your hands. You have put all things in subjection under his feet.   (Hebrews 2:6–8)

Aid to the Seed of Abraham

Inasmuch then as the children have partaken of flesh and blood, He Himself likewise shared in the same, that through death He might destroy him who had the power of death, that is, the devil, and release those who through fear of death were all their lifetime subject to bondage. For indeed He does not give aid to angels, but He does give aid to the seed of Abraham.   (Hebrews 2:14–16)

We Christians Are God's House

But Christ, God's faithful Son, is in complete charge of God's house. And we Christians are God's house—he lives in us!—if we keep up our courage firm to the end, and our joy and our trust in the Lord.   (Hebrews 3:6 TLB)

Sharper than Any Two-edged Sword

For the word of God is living and powerful, and sharper than any two-edged sword, piercing even to the division of soul and spirit, and of joints and marrow, and is a discerner of the thoughts and intents of the heart.

(Hebrews 4:12)

Sharper than the Sharpest Dagger

For whatever God says to us is full of living power: it is sharper than the sharpest dagger, cutting swift and deep into our innermost thoughts and desires with all their parts, exposing us for what we really are.

(Hebrews 4:12 TLB)

Help in Time of Need

Let us therefore come boldly to the throne of grace, that we may obtain mercy and find grace to help in time of need.

(Hebrews 4:16)

Coming Just When We Need It

For we do not have a High Priest Who is unable to understand and sympathize and have a shared feeling with our weaknesses and infirmities and liability to the assaults of temptation, but One Who has been tempted in every respect as we are, yet without sinning. Let us then fearlessly and confidently and boldly draw near to the throne of grace (the throne of God's unmerited favor to us sinners, that we may receive mercy [for our failures] and find grace to help in good time for every need [appropriate help and well-timed help, coming just when we need it].

(Hebrews 4:15–16 AMP)

You Are My Son

You are My Son; today I have begotten You.   (Hebrews 5:5 AMP)

Author of Eternal Salvation

And having been perfected, He became the author of eternal salvation to all who obey Him.

(Hebrews 5:9)

I Will Bless You

For when God made a promise to Abraham, because He could swear by no one greater, He swore by Himself, saying, "Surely blessing I will bless you, and multiplying I will multiply you."

(Hebrews 6:13–14)

It Is Impossible for God to Tell a Lie

God also bound himself with an oath, so that those he promised to help would be perfectly sure and never need to wonder whether he might change his plans. He has given us both his promise and his oath, two things we can completely count on, for it is impossible for God to tell a lie.

(Hebrews 6:17–18 TLB)

Better Covenant

"The LORD has sworn and will not relent, 'You are a priest forever according to the order of Melchizedek'"…by so much more Jesus has become a surety of a better covenant. (Hebrews 7:21–22)

Lives to Make Intercession for Them

Therefore He is also able to save to the uttermost those who come to God through Him, since He always lives to make intercession for them. (Hebrews 7:25)

I Will Write Them on Their Hearts

"Behold, the days are coming, says the LORD, when I will make a new covenant with the house of Israel and with the house of Judah....For this is the covenant that I will make with the house of Israel after those days, says the LORD: I will put My laws in their mind and write them on their hearts; and I will be their God, and they shall be My people." (Hebrews 8:8, 10)

Remember No More

For I will be merciful to their unrighteousness, and their sins and their lawless deeds I will remember no more. (Hebrews 8:12)

To Bring to Full Salvation

Even so it is that Christ, having been offered to take upon Himself and bear as a burden the sins of many once and once for all, will appear a second time, not to carry any burden of sin nor to deal with sin, but to bring to full salvation those who are [eagerly, constantly, and patiently] waiting for and expecting Him. (Hebrews 9:28 AMP)

Substance of Things Hoped For

Now faith is the substance of things hoped for, the evidence of things not seen. (Hebrews 11:1)

The Confident Assurance

What is faith? It is the confident assurance that something we want is going to happen. It is the certainty that what we hope for is waiting for us, even though we cannot see it up ahead.
(Hebrews 11:1 TLB)

Faith Perceiving as Real Fact

Now faith is the assurance (the confirmation, the title deed) of the things [we] hope for, being the proof of things [we] do not see and the conviction of their reality [faith perceiving as real fact what is not revealed to the senses].
(Hebrews 11:1 AMP)

All Things Were Made at God's Command

By faith—by believing God—we know that the world and the stars—in fact, all things—were made at God's command; and that they were all made from things that can't be seen.
(Hebrews 11:3 TLB)

He Is a Rewarder

But without faith it is impossible to please Him, for he who comes to God must believe that He is, and that He is a rewarder of those who diligently seek Him.
(Hebrews 11:6)

True to His Word

Because of faith also Sarah herself received physical power to conceive a child, even when she was long past the age for it, because she considered [God] Who had given her the promise to be reliable and trustworthy and true to His word.
(Hebrews 11:11 AMP)

The Innumerable Sands on the Seashore

So from one man, though he was physically as good as dead, there have sprung descendants whose number is as the stars of heaven and as countless as the innumerable sands on the seashore.

(Hebrews 11:12 AMP)

At the Right Hand of the Throne of God

Therefore we also, since we are surrounded by so great a cloud of witnesses, let us lay aside every weight, and the sin which so easily ensnares us, and let us run with endurance the race that is set before us, looking unto Jesus, the author and finisher of our faith, who for the joy that was set before Him endured the cross, despising the shame, and has sat down at the right hand of the throne of God.

(Hebrews 12:1–2)

Right Standing with God

For [our earthly fathers] disciplined us for only a short period of time and chastised us as seemed proper and good to them; but He disciplines us for our certain good, that we may become sharers in His own holiness. For the time being no discipline brings joy, but seems grievous and painful; but afterwards it yields peaceable fruit of righteousness to those who have been trained by it [a harvest of fruit which consists in righteousness—in conformity to God's will in purpose, thought, and action, resulting in right living and right standing with God].

(Hebrews 12:10–11 AMP)

God Is a Consuming Fire

Now this expression, Yet once more, indicates the final removal and transformation of all [that can be] shaken—that is, of that which has been created—in order that what cannot be shaken may remain and continue. Let us therefore, receiving a kingdom that is firm and stable and cannot be shaken, offer to God pleasing service and acceptable worship, with modesty and pious care and godly fear and awe; for our God [is indeed] a consuming fire.   (Hebrews 12:27–29 AMP)

I Will Not Fear

For He Himself has said, "I will never leave you nor forsake you." So we may boldly say: "The LORD is my helper; I will not fear. What can man do to me?"   (Hebrews 13:5–6)

Forever

Jesus Christ is the same yesterday, today, and forever.   (Hebrews 13:8)

Make You Complete

Now may the God of peace who brought up our LORD Jesus from the dead, that great Shepherd of the sheep, through the blood of the everlasting covenant, make you complete in every good work to do His will, working in you what is well pleasing in His sight, through Jesus Christ, to whom be glory forever and ever. Amen.   (Hebrews 13:20–21)

Promises from Hosea

The Living God

You are sons of the living God. (Hosea 1:10)

His Gift of Salvation upon You

Sow for yourselves according to righteousness (uprightness and right standing with God); reap according to mercy and loving-kindness. Break up your uncultivated ground, for it is time to seek the Lord, to inquire for and of Him, and to require His favor, till He comes and teaches you righteousness and rains His righteous gift of salvation upon you. (Hosea 10:12 AMP)

No Savior besides Me

Yet I am the LORD your God ever since the land of Egypt, and you shall know no God but Me; for there is no Savior besides Me. (Hosea 13:4)

Walk in Them

For the ways of the LORD are right; the righteous walk in them, but transgressors stumble in them. (Hosea 14:9)

Promises from Isaiah

They Shall Be As White as Snow

Though your sins are like scarlet, they shall be as white as snow; though they are red like crimson, they shall be as wool. If you are willing and obedient, you shall eat the good of the land.   (Isaiah 1:18–19)

What a Reward

But all is well for the godly man. Tell him, "What a reward you are going to get!"   (Isaiah 3:10 TLB)

Great Prosecuting Attorney

The Lord stands up! He is the great Prosecuting Attorney presenting his case against his people!
(Isaiah 3:13 TLB)

Whole Earth Is Full of His Glory

I saw the Lord sitting on a throne, high and lifted up, and the train of His robe filled the temple. Above it stood seraphim; each one had six wings: with two he covered his face, with two he covered his feet, and with two he flew. And one cried to another and said: "Holy, holy, holy is the LORD of hosts; the whole earth is full of His glory!"
(Isaiah 6:1–3)

Shall Call His Name Immanuel

Therefore the Lord Himself will give you a sign: Behold, the virgin shall conceive and bear a Son, and shall call His name Immanuel. (Isaiah 7:14)

From That Time Forward, Even Forever

For unto us a Child is born, unto us a Son is given; and the government will be upon His shoulder. And His name will be called Wonderful, Counselor, Mighty God, Everlasting Father, Prince of Peace. Of the increase of His government and peace there will be no end, upon the throne of David and over His kingdom, to order it and establish it with judgment and justice from that time forward, even forever. The zeal of the LORD of hosts will perform this. (Isaiah 9:6–7)

Great Is the Holy One of Israel

"Behold, God is my salvation, I will trust and not be afraid; 'For YAH, the LORD, is my strength and song; He also has become my salvation.'" Therefore with joy you will draw water from the wells of salvation. And in that day you will say: "Praise the LORD, call upon His name; declare His deeds among the peoples, make mention that His name is exalted. Sing to the LORD, for He has done excellent things; this is known in all the earth. Cry out and shout, O inhabitant of Zion, for great is the Holy One of Israel in your midst!" (Isaiah 12:2–6)

Respect for the Holy One of Israel

In that day a man will look to his Maker, and his eyes will have respect for the Holy One of Israel. (Isaiah 17:7)

The Rock of Ages

You will keep him in perfect peace, whose mind is stayed on You, because he trusts in You. Trust in the LORD forever, for in YAH, the LORD, is everlasting strength. (Isaiah 26:3–4)

Eyes, Ears, Heart, Tongue

The eyes of those who see will not be dim, and the ears of those who hear will listen. Also the heart of the rash will understand knowledge, and the tongue of the stammerers will be ready to speak plainly. (Isaiah 32:3–4)

He Will Come and Save You

Strengthen the weak hands and make firm the feeble and tottering knees. Say to those who are of a fearful and hasty heart, Be strong, fear not! Behold, your God will come with vengeance; with the recompense of God He will come and save you. (Isaiah 35:3–4 AMP)

Highway of Holiness

Then the eyes of the blind shall be opened, and the ears of the deaf shall be unstopped. Then the lame shall leap like a deer, and the tongue of the dumb sing. For waters shall burst forth in the wilderness, and streams in the desert. The parched ground shall become a pool, and the thirsty land springs of water....A highway shall be there, and a road, and it shall be called the Highway of Holiness. (Isaiah 35:5–8)

Sorrow and Sighing Shall Flee Away

And the ransomed of the LORD shall return, and come to Zion with singing, with everlasting joy on their heads. They shall obtain joy and gladness, and sorrow and sighing shall flee away.
(Isaiah 35:10)

You Have Made Heaven and Earth

O LORD of hosts, God of Israel, the One who dwells between the cherubim, You are God, You alone, of all the kingdoms of the earth. You have made heaven and earth.
(Isaiah 37:16)

The Mouth of the Lord Has Spoken

Prepare the way of the LORD; make straight in the desert a highway for our God. Every valley shall be exalted and every mountain and hill brought low; the crooked places shall be made straight and the rough places smooth; the glory of the LORD shall be revealed, and all flesh shall see it together; for the mouth of the LORD has spoken.
(Isaiah 40:3–5)

Word of Our God Stands

The grass withers, the flower fades, but the word of our God stands forever.
(Isaiah 40:8)

He Increases Strength

Have you not known? Have you not heard? The everlasting God, the Lord, the Creator of the ends of the earth, does not faint or grow weary; there is no searching of His understanding. He gives power to the faint and weary, and to him who has no might He increases strength [causing it to multiply and making it to abound].
(Isaiah 40:28–29 AMP)

Those Who Wait on the Lord

Those who wait on the Lord shall renew their strength; they shall mount up with wings like eagles, they shall run and not be weary, they shall walk and not faint.

(Isaiah 40:31)

I Will Uphold You

Fear not, for I am with you; be not dismayed, for I am your God. I will strengthen you, yes, I will help you, I will uphold you with My righteous right hand.

(Isaiah 41:10)

I Will Help You

I, the Lord your God, will hold your right hand, saying to you, "Fear not, I will help you."

(Isaiah 41:13)

I Tell You of Them

Behold, the former things have come to pass, and new things I declare; before they spring forth I tell you of them.

(Isaiah 42:9)

I Will Not Forsake Them

I will bring the blind by a way they did not know; I will lead them in paths they have not known. I will make darkness light before them, and crooked places straight. These things I will do for them, and not forsake them.

(Isaiah 42:16)

I Am the Lord Your God

Fear not, for I have redeemed you; I have called you by your name; you are Mine. When you pass through the waters, I will be with you; and through the rivers, they shall not overflow you. When you walk through the fire, you shall not be burned, nor shall the flame scorch you. For I am the LORD your God, the Holy One of Israel, your Savior. (Isaiah 43:1–3)

I Have Created for My Glory

Fear not, for I am with you; I will bring your descendants from the east, and gather you from the west; I will say to the north, "Give them up!" And to the south, "Do not keep them back!" Bring My sons from afar, and My daughters from the ends of the earth; everyone who is called by My name, whom I have created for My glory; I have formed him, yes, I have made him.   (Isaiah 43:5–7)

I Am God

"You are My witnesses," says the LORD, "and My servant whom I have chosen, that you may know and believe Me, and understand that I am He. Before Me there was no God formed, nor shall there be after Me. I, even I, am the LORD, and besides Me there is no savior. I have declared and saved, I have proclaimed, and there was no foreign god among you; therefore you are My witnesses," says the LORD, "that I am God."   (Isaiah 43:10–12)

Now It Shall Spring Forth

Do not remember the former things, nor consider the things of old. Behold, I will do a new thing, now it shall spring forth.   (Isaiah 43:18–19)

Blessing on Your Offspring

For I will pour water on him who is thirsty, and floods on the dry ground; I will pour My Spirit on your descendants, and My blessing on your offspring. (Isaiah 44:3)

I Am

I am the First and I am the Last; besides Me there is no God. (Isaiah 44:6)

Who Makes All Things

I am the LORD, who makes all things, who stretches out the heavens all alone, who spreads abroad the earth by Myself. (Isaiah 44:24)

Hidden Riches of Secret Places

I will go before you and level the mountains [to make the crooked places straight]; I will break in pieces the doors of bronze and cut asunder the bars of iron. And I will give you the treasures of darkness and hidden riches of secret places, that you may know that it is I, the Lord, the God of Israel, Who calls you by your name. (Isaiah 45:2–3 AMP)

There Is No God besides Me

I am the Lord, and there is no one else; there is no God besides Me. (Isaiah 45:5 AMP)

I Am God

Look to Me, and be saved, all you ends of the earth! For I am God, and there is no other. (Isaiah 45:22)

None like Me

Remember the former things of old, for I am God,…and there is none like Me. (Isaiah 46:9)

First—Also the Last

I am He, I am the First, I am also the Last. Indeed My hand has laid the foundation of the earth, and My right hand has stretched out the heavens; when I call to them, they stand up together.

(Isaiah 48:12–13)

Who Leads You by the Way

I am the LORD your God, who teaches you to profit, who leads you by the way you should go.

(Isaiah 48:17)

I Have Inscribed You

See, I have inscribed you on the palms of My hands. (Isaiah 49:16)

I Will Save Your Children

For I will fight those who fight you, and I will save your children. (Isaiah 49:25 TLB)

My Righteousness Will Not Be Abolished

Lift up your eyes to the heavens, and look on the earth beneath. For the heavens will vanish away like smoke, the earth will grow old like a garment, and those who dwell in it will die in like manner; but My salvation will be forever, and My righteousness will not be abolished. (Isaiah 51:6)

Shall Obtain Joy and Gladness

So the ransomed of the LORD shall return, and come to Zion with singing, with everlasting joy on their heads. They shall obtain joy and gladness; sorrow and sighing shall flee away.   (Isaiah 51:11)

Your God Reigns

How beautiful upon the mountains are the feet of him who brings good news, who proclaims peace, who brings glad tidings of good things, who proclaims salvation, who says to Zion, "Your God reigns!"   (Isaiah 52:7)

Shall Stand Very High

Behold, My Servant shall deal wisely and shall prosper; He shall be exalted and extolled, and shall stand very high.   (Isaiah 52:13 AMP)

By His Stripes We Are Healed

Surely He has borne our griefs and carried our sorrows; yet we esteemed Him stricken, smitten by God, and afflicted. But He was wounded for our transgressions, He was bruised for our iniquities; the chastisement for our peace was upon Him, and by His stripes we are healed.   (Isaiah 53:4–5)

Your Descendants Inherit the Nations

Enlarge the place of your tent, and let them stretch out the curtains of your dwellings; do not spare; lengthen your cords, and strengthen your stakes. For you shall expand to the right and to the left, and your descendants will inherit the nations.   (Isaiah 54:2–3)

I Will Have Mercy

"With everlasting kindness I will have mercy on you," says the LORD, your Redeemer.   (Isaiah 54:8)

You Shall Be Established

All your children shall be taught by the LORD, and great shall be the peace of your children. In righteousness you shall be established; you shall be far from oppression, for you shall not fear; and from terror, for it shall not come near you.   (Isaiah 54:13–14)

I Impart to Them

"No weapon formed against you shall prosper, and every tongue which rises against you in judgment you shall condemn. This is the heritage of the servants of the LORD, and their righteousness is from Me," says the LORD.   (Isaiah 54:17)

Everlasting Covenant

Incline your ear, and come to Me. Hear, and your soul shall live; and I will make an everlasting covenant with you.   (Isaiah 55:3)

He Will Abundantly Pardon

Seek the LORD while He may be found, call upon Him while He is near. Let the wicked forsake his way, and the unrighteous man his thoughts; let him return to the LORD, and He will have mercy on him; and to our God, for He will abundantly pardon.   (Isaiah 55:6–7)

My Ways Higher than Your Ways

"For My thoughts are not your thoughts, nor are your ways My ways," says the LORD. "For as the heavens are higher than the earth, so are My ways higher than your ways, and My thoughts than your thoughts." (Isaiah 55:8–9)

Shall Not Return to Me Void

For as the rain comes down, and the snow from heaven, and do not return there, but water the earth, and make it bring forth and bud, that it may give seed to the sower and bread to the eater, so shall My word be that goes forth from My mouth; it shall not return to Me void, but it shall accomplish what I please, and it shall prosper in the thing for which I sent it. (Isaiah 55:10–11)

Trees Shall Clap Their Hands

For you shall go out with joy, and be led out with peace; the mountains and the hills shall break forth into singing before you, and all the trees of the field shall clap their hands. (Isaiah 55:12)

A House of Prayer

Everyone who keeps from defiling the Sabbath, and holds fast My covenant; even them I will bring to My holy mountain, and make them joyful in My house of prayer. Their burnt offerings and their sacrifices will be accepted on My altar; for My house shall be called a house of prayer for all nations. (Isaiah 56:6–7)

Shall Inherit

He who puts his trust in Me shall possess the land, and shall inherit My holy mountain. (Isaiah 57:13)

To Revive the Heart

For thus says the High and Lofty One who inhabits eternity, whose name is Holy: "I dwell in the high and holy place, with him who has a contrite and humble spirit, to revive the spirit of the humble, and to revive the heart of the contrite ones." (Isaiah 57:15)

I Will Heal Him

"I create the fruit of the lips: Peace, peace to him who is far off and to him who is near," says the LORD, "and I will heal him." (Isaiah 57:19)

Here I Am

Then your light shall break forth like the morning, your healing shall spring forth speedily, and your righteousness shall go before you; the glory of the LORD shall be your rear guard. Then you shall call, and the LORD will answer; you shall cry, and He will say, 'Here I am.' "If you take away the yoke from your midst, the pointing of the finger, and speaking wickedness,…then your light shall dawn in the darkness." (Isaiah 58:8–9)

Waters Do Not Fail

The LORD will guide you continually, and satisfy your soul in drought, and strengthen your bones; you shall be like a watered garden, and like a spring of water, whose waters do not fail. (Isaiah 58:11)

Hand Is Not Shortened

Behold, the LORD's hand is not shortened, that it cannot save; nor His ear heavy, that it cannot hear. (Isaiah 59:1)

Lord Will Lift Up a Standard

When the enemy comes in like a flood, the Spirit of the LORD will lift up a standard against him.

(Isaiah 59:19)

Shall Not Depart from Your Mouth

"As for Me," says the LORD, "this is My covenant with them: My Spirit who is upon you, and My words which I have put in your mouth, shall not depart from your mouth, nor from the mouth of your descendants, nor from the mouth of your descendants' descendants," says the LORD, "from this time and forevermore."

(Isaiah 59:21)

His Glory Will Be Seen upon You

Arise, shine; for your light has come! And the glory of the LORD is risen upon you. For behold, the darkness shall cover the earth, and deep darkness the people; but the LORD will arise over you, and His glory will be seen upon you.

(Isaiah 60:1–2)

Gates Shall Be Open Continually

And your gates shall be open continually, they shall not be shut day or night, that men may bring to you the wealth of the nations—and their kings led in procession [your voluntary captives].

(Isaiah 60:11 AMP)

Lord Will Be Your Everlasting Light

The sun shall no longer be your light by day, nor for brightness shall the moon give light to you; but the LORD will be to you an everlasting light, and your God your glory. Your sun shall no longer go down, nor shall your moon withdraw itself; for the LORD will be your everlasting light, and the days of your mourning shall be ended. (Isaiah 60:19–20)

Healing, Liberty, and Joy

The Spirit of the Lord GOD is upon Me, because the LORD has anointed Me to preach good tidings to the poor; He has sent Me to heal the brokenhearted, to proclaim liberty to the captives, and the opening of the prison to those who are bound; to proclaim the acceptable year of the LORD, and the day of vengeance of our God; to comfort all who mourn, to console those who mourn in Zion, to give them beauty for ashes, the oil of joy for mourning, the garment of praise for the spirit of heaviness; that they may be called trees of righteousness, the planting of the LORD, that He may be glorified. (Isaiah 61:1–3)

The Glory Shall Be Yours

But you shall be called the priests of the Lord; people will speak of you as the ministers of our God. You shall eat the wealth of the nations, and the glory [once that of your captors] shall be yours. (Isaiah 61:6 AMP)

He Has Covered Me

I will greatly rejoice in the LORD, my soul shall be joyful in my God; for He has clothed me with the garments of salvation, He has covered me with the robe of righteousness. (Isaiah 61:10)

Promises from Isaiah

Righteousness and Praise Spring Forth

For as the earth brings forth its bud, as the garden causes the things that are sown in it to spring forth, so the Lord GOD will cause righteousness and praise to spring forth before all the nations.

(Isaiah 61:11)

A Royal Diadem

You shall be called by a new name, which the mouth of the LORD will name. You shall also be a crown of glory in the hand of the LORD, and a royal diadem in the hand of your God.   (Isaiah 62:2–3)

God Shall Rejoice over You

And as the bridegroom rejoices over the bride, so shall your God rejoice over you.   (Isaiah 62:5)

The Work of Your Hand

But now, O LORD, You are our Father; we are the clay, and You our potter; and all we are the work of Your hand.   (Isaiah 64:8)

New Heavens

For behold, I create new heavens and a new earth; and the former shall not be remembered or come to mind.   (Isaiah 65:17)

Before They Call

It shall come to pass that before they call, I will answer; and while they are still speaking, I will hear.   (Isaiah 65:24)

On This One Will I Look

Thus says the LORD: "Heaven is My throne, and earth is My footstool. Where is the house that you will build Me? And where is the place of My rest? For all those things My hand has made, and all those things exist," says the LORD. "But on this one will I look: On him who is poor and of a contrite spirit, and who trembles at My word."

(Isaiah 66:1–2)

Come and See My Glory

For I know their works and their thoughts. It shall be that I will gather all nations and tongues; and they shall come and see My glory.

(Isaiah 66:18)

Your Name

"For as the new heavens and the new earth which I will make shall remain before Me," says the LORD, "so shall your descendants and your name remain."

(Isaiah 66:22)

Promises from James

It Will Be Given to Him

If any of you lacks wisdom, he should ask God, who gives generously to all without finding fault, and it will be given to him.

(James 1:5 NIV)

Receive the Crown of Life

Blessed is the man who perseveres under trial, because when he has stood the test, he will receive the crown of life that God has promised to those who love him.   (James 1:12 NIV)

First Children in His New Family

Whatever is good and perfect comes to us from God, the Creator of all light, and he shines forever without change or shadow. And it was a happy day for him when he gave us our new lives, through the truth of his Word, and we became, as it were, the first children in his new family. (James 1:17–18 TLB)

Blessed in What He Does

But the man who looks intently into the perfect law that gives freedom, and continues to do this, not forgetting what he has heard, but doing it—he will be blessed in what he does.   (James 1:25 NIV)

The Kingdom of Heaven Is Theirs

God has chosen poor people to be rich in faith, and the kingdom of Heaven is theirs, for that is the gift God has promised to all those who love him.   (James 2:5 TLB)

Justified by What He Does

"Abraham believed God, and it was credited to him as righteousness," and he was called God's friend. You see that a person is justified by what he does and not by faith alone.   (James 2:23–24 NIV)

Harvest of Righteousness

But the wisdom that comes from heaven is first of all pure; then peace-loving, considerate, submissive, full of mercy and good fruit, impartial and sincere. Peacemakers who sow in peace raise a harvest of righteousness.

(James 3:17–18 NIV)

Grace to the Humble

God opposes the proud but gives grace to the humble.

(James 4:6)

He Will Come Near to You

Submit yourselves, then, to God. Resist the devil, and he will flee from you. Come near to God and he will come near to you.

(James 4:7–8 NIV)

He Will Lift You Up

Change your laughter to mourning and your joy to gloom. Humble yourselves before the Lord, and he will lift you up.

(James 4:9–10 NIV)

Full of Compassion and Mercy

The Lord is full of compassion and mercy.

(James 5:11 NIV)

The Prayer of a Righteous Man Is Powerful

Is any one of you in trouble? He should pray. Is anyone happy? Let him sing songs of praise. Is any one of you sick? He should call the elders of the church to pray over him and anoint him with oil in the name of the Lord. And the prayer offered in faith will make the sick person well; the Lord will raise him up. If he has sinned, he will be forgiven. Therefore confess your sins to each other and pray for each other so that you may be healed. The prayer of a righteous man is powerful and effective. (James 5:13–16 NIV)

Dynamic in Its Working

The earnest (heartfelt, continued) prayer of a righteous man makes tremendous power available [dynamic in its working]. (James 5:16 AMP)

Promises from Jeremiah

Before You Were Born

Before I formed you in the womb I knew you; before you were born I sanctified you. (Jeremiah 1:5)

I Am with You to Deliver You

"For you shall go to all to whom I send you, and whatever I command you, you shall speak. Do not be afraid of their faces, for I am with you to deliver you," says the LORD. (Jeremiah 1:7–8)

To Build and to Plant

Behold, I have put My words in your mouth. See, I have this day set you over the nations and over the kingdoms, to root out and to pull down, to destroy and to throw down, to build and to plant.

(Jeremiah 1:9–10)

They Shall Not Prevail

"They will fight against you, but they shall not prevail against you. For I am with you," says the LORD, "to deliver you."

(Jeremiah 1:19)

A Seed of Highest Quality

I had planted you a noble vine, a seed of highest quality.

(Jeremiah 2:21)

They Cannot Pass over It

Will you not tremble at My presence, who have placed the sand as the bound of the sea, by a perpetual decree, that it cannot pass beyond it? And though its waves toss to and fro, yet they cannot prevail; though they roar, yet they cannot pass over it.

(Jeremiah 5:22)

Rest for Your Souls

Thus says the LORD: "Stand in the ways and see, and ask for the old paths, where the good way is, and walk in it; then you will find rest for your souls."

(Jeremiah 6:16)

Everlasting King

But the LORD is the true God; He is the living God and the everlasting King.   (Jeremiah 10:10)

Wind out of His Treasuries

He has made the earth by His power, He has established the world by His wisdom, and has stretched out the heavens at His discretion. When He utters His voice, there is a multitude of waters in the heavens: "And He causes the vapors to ascend from the ends of the earth. He makes lightning for the rain, He brings the wind out of His treasuries."   (Jeremiah 10:12–13)

I Will Be Your God

Obey My voice, and do according to all that I command you; so shall you be My people, and I will be your God.   (Jeremiah 11:4)

Will Not Be Anxious

Blessed is the man who trusts in the LORD, and whose hope is the LORD. For he shall be like a tree planted by the waters, which spreads out its roots by the river, and will not fear when heat comes; but its leaf will be green, and will not be anxious in the year of drought, nor will cease from yielding fruit.   (Jeremiah 17:7–8)

You Are My Praise

Heal me, O LORD, and I shall be healed; save me, and I shall be saved, for You are my praise.   (Jeremiah 17:14)

Fill Heaven and Earth

"Am I a God near at hand," says the LORD, "and not a God afar off? Can anyone hide himself in secret places, so I shall not see him?" says the LORD; "Do I not fill heaven and earth?" says the LORD.

(Jeremiah 23:23–24)

Breaks the Rock in Pieces

"The prophet who has a dream, let him tell a dream; and he who has My word, let him speak My word faithfully. What is the chaff to the wheat?" says the LORD. "Is not My word like a fire?" says the LORD, "and like a hammer that breaks the rock in pieces?"

(Jeremiah 23:28–29)

With Their Whole Heart

I will give them a heart to know Me, that I am the LORD; and they shall be My people, and I will be their God, for they shall return to Me with their whole heart.

(Jeremiah 24:7)

By My Great Power

I have made the earth, the man and the beast that are on the ground, by My great power and by My outstretched arm, and have given it to whom it seemed proper to Me.

(Jeremiah 27:5)

With All Your Heart

For I know the thoughts that I think toward you, says the LORD, thoughts of peace and not of evil, to give you a future and a hope. Then you will call upon Me and go and pray to Me, and I will listen to you. And you will seek Me and find Me, when you search for Me with all your heart. I will be found by you, says the LORD.

(Jeremiah 29:11–14)

Restore Health

"For I will restore health to you and heal you of your wounds," says the Lord. (Jeremiah 30:17)

I Will Be Your God

You shall be My people, and I will be your God. (Jeremiah 30:22)

An Everlasting Love

I have loved you with an everlasting love. (Jeremiah 31:3)

My People Shall Be Satisfied

My people shall be satisfied with My goodness, says the Lord. (Jeremiah 31:14)

Their Sin I Will Remember No More

But this is the covenant that I will make with the house of Israel after those days, says the Lord: I will put My law in their minds, and write it on their hearts; and I will be their God, and they shall be My people. No more shall every man teach his neighbor, and every man his brother, saying, "Know the Lord," for they all shall know Me, from the least of them to the greatest of them, says the Lord. For I will forgive their iniquity, and their sin I will remember no more. (Jeremiah 31:33–34)

The Lord of Hosts

Thus says the Lord, who gives the sun for a light by day, the ordinances of the moon and the stars for a light by night, who disturbs the sea, and its waves roar (The Lord of hosts is His name). (Jeremiah 31:35)

There Is Nothing Too Hard for You

Ah, Lord GOD! Behold, You have made the heavens and the earth by Your great power and outstretched arm. There is nothing too hard for You. (Jeremiah 32:17)

Anything Too Hard for Me?

Behold, I am the LORD, the God of all flesh. Is there anything too hard for Me? (Jeremiah 32:27)

I Will Not Turn Away

They shall be My people, and I will be their God; then I will give them one heart and one way, that they may fear Me forever, for the good of them and their children after them. And I will make an everlasting covenant with them, that I will not turn away from doing them good; but I will put My fear in their hearts so that they will not depart from Me. (Jeremiah 32:38–40)

Great and Mighty Things

Thus says the LORD who made it, the LORD who formed it to establish it (the LORD is His name): "Call to Me, and I will answer you, and show you great and mighty things, which you do not know." (Jeremiah 33:2–3)

Peace and Truth

Behold, I will bring it health and healing; I will heal them and reveal to them the abundance of peace and truth. (Jeremiah 33:6)

His Mercy Endures Forever

Praise the LORD of hosts, for the LORD is good, for His mercy endures forever. (Jeremiah 33:11)

Promises from Job

Sudden Disaster

Those who turn from God may be successful for the moment, but then comes sudden disaster.

(Job 5:3 TLB)

No Evil Can Touch You

How enviable the man whom God corrects! Oh, do not despise the chastening of the Lord when you sin. For though he wounds, he binds and heals again. He will deliver you again and again, so that no evil can touch you. (Job 5:17–19 TLB)

You'll Not Be Harvested until It's Time

He will keep you from death in famine, and from the power of the sword in time of war. You will be safe from slander; no need to fear the future. You shall laugh at war and famine; wild animals will leave you alone. Dangerous animals will be at peace with you. You need not worry about your home while you are gone; nothing shall be stolen from your barns. Your sons shall become important men; your descendants shall be as numerous as grass! You shall live a long, good life; like standing grain, you'll not be harvested until it's time! (Job 5:20–26 TLB)

God Will Not Cast Away a Good Man

A man without God is trusting in a spider's web. Everything he counts on will collapse. If he counts on his home for security, it won't last. At dawn he seems so strong and virile, like a green plant; his branches spread across the garden. His roots are in the stream, down among the stones. But when he disappears, he isn't even missed! That is all he can look forward to! And others spring up from the earth to replace him! But look! God will not cast away a good man, nor prosper evildoers. He will yet fill your mouth with laughter and your lips with shouts of joy.   (Job 8:14–21 TLB)

Wider than the Sea

His Spirit is broader than the earth and wider than the sea. If he rushes in and makes an arrest, and calls the court to order, who is going to stop him? For he knows perfectly all the faults and sins of mankind; he sees all sin without searching.   (Job 11:9–11 TLB)

The Breath of all Mankind

For the soul of every living thing is in the hand of God, and the breath of all mankind.   (Job 12:10 TLB)

True Wisdom

True wisdom and power are God's.   (Job 12:13 TLB)

Higher than the Stars

God is so great—higher than the heavens, higher than the stars.   (Job 22:12 TLB)

God Stretches Out Heaven

God stretches out heaven over empty space, and hangs the earth upon nothing. He wraps the rain in his thick clouds and the clouds are not split by the weight. He shrouds his throne with his clouds. He sets a boundary for the ocean, yes, and a boundary for the day and for the night. The pillars of heaven tremble at his rebuke. And by his power the sea grows calm; he is skilled at crushing its pride! The heavens are made beautiful by his Spirit; he pierces the swiftly gliding serpent. These are some of the minor things he does, merely a whisper of his power. Who then can withstand his thunder?

(Job 26:7–14 TLB)

The Breath of the Almighty Gives Me Life

The Spirit of God has made me, and the breath of the Almighty gives me life.　　(Job 33:4 TLB)

God Speaks Again and Again

For God speaks again and again, in dreams, in visions of the night when deep sleep falls on men as they lie on their beds. He opens their ears in times like that, and gives them wisdom and instruction, causing them to change their minds, and keeping them from pride, and warning them of the penalties of sin, and keeping them from falling into some trap.　　(Job 33:14–18 TLB)

God Is Never Wicked or Unjust

God is never wicked or unjust. He alone has authority over the earth and dispenses justice for the world. If God were to withdraw his Spirit, all life would disappear and mankind would turn again to dust.

(Job 34:12–15 TLB)

They Will Be Blessed with Prosperity

God is almighty and yet does not despise anyone! And he is perfect in his understanding. He does not reward the wicked with his blessings, but gives them their full share of punishment. He does not ignore the good men but honors them by placing them upon eternal, kingly thrones. If troubles come upon them, and they are enslaved and afflicted, then he takes the trouble to point out to them the reason, what they have done that is wrong, or how they have behaved proudly. He helps them hear his instruction to turn away from their sin. If they listen and obey him, then they will be blessed with prosperity throughout their lives. (Job 36:5–11 TLB)

We Feel His Presence in the Thunder

God is so great that we cannot begin to know him. No one can begin to understand eternity. He draws up the water vapor and then distills it into rain, which the skies pour down. Can anyone really understand the spreading of the clouds, and the thunders within? See how he spreads the lightning around him, and blankets the tops of the mountains. By his fantastic powers in nature he punishes or blesses the people, giving them food in abundance. He fills his hands with lightning bolts. He hurls each at its target. We feel his presence in the thunder. May all sinners be warned. (Job 36:26–33 TLB)

The Greatness of His Power

My heart trembles at this. Listen, listen to the thunder of his voice. It rolls across the heavens and his lightning flashes out in every direction. Afterwards comes the roaring of the thunder—the tremendous voice of his majesty. His voice is glorious in the thunder. We cannot comprehend the greatness of his power. For he directs the snow, the showers, and storm to fall upon the earth. Man's work stops at such a time, so that all men everywhere may recognize his power. The wild animals hide in the rocks or in their dens. From the south comes the rain; from the north, the cold. God blows upon the rivers, and even the widest torrents freeze. He loads the clouds with moisture and they send forth his lightning. The lightning bolts are directed by his hand, and do whatever he commands throughout the earth. He sends the storms as punishment, or, in his lovingkindness, to encourage. Listen, O Job, stop and consider the wonderful miracles of God. Do you know how God controls all nature, and causes the lightning to flash forth from the clouds? Do you understand the balancing of the clouds with wonderful perfection and skill? Do you know why you become warm when the south wind is blowing and everything is still? Can you spread out the gigantic mirror of the skies as he does? (Job 37:1–18 TLB)

Men Everywhere Fear Him

For as we cannot look at the sun for its brightness when the winds have cleared away the clouds, neither can we gaze at the terrible majesty of God breaking forth upon us from heaven, clothed in dazzling splendor. We cannot imagine the power of the Almighty, and yet he is so just and merciful that he does not destroy us. No wonder men everywhere fear him! (Job 37:21–24 TLB)

Who Is Wise Enough

Where were you when I laid the foundations of the earth? Tell me, if you know so much. Do you know how its dimensions were determined, and who did the surveying? What supports its foundations, and who laid its cornerstone, as the morning stars sang together and all the angels shouted for joy? Who decreed the boundaries of the seas when they gushed from the depths? Who clothed them with clouds and thick darkness, and barred them by limiting their shores, and said, "Thus far and no farther shall you come, and here shall your proud waves stop!"? Have you ever once commanded the morning to appear, and caused the dawn to rise in the east? Have you ever told the daylight to spread to the ends of the earth, to end the night's wickedness? Have you ever robed the dawn in red, and disturbed the haunts of wicked men and stopped the arm raised to strike? Have you explored the springs from which the seas come, or walked in the sources of their depths? Has the location of the gates of Death been revealed to you? Do you realize the extent of the earth? Tell me about it if you know! Where does the light come from, and how do you get there? Or tell me about the darkness. Where does it come from? Can you find its boundaries, or go to its source? But of course you know all this! For you were born before it was all created, and you are so very experienced! Have you visited the treasuries of the snow, or seen where hail is made and stored? For I have reserved it for the time when I will need it in war. Where is the path to the distribution point of light? Where is the home of the east wind? Who dug the valleys for the torrents of rain? Who laid out the path for the lightning, causing the rain to fall upon the barren deserts, so that the parched and barren ground is satisfied with water, and tender grass springs up? Has the rain a father? Where does dew come from? Who is the mother of the ice and frost? For the water changes and turns to ice, as hard as rock. Can you hold back the stars? Can you restrain Orion or Pleiades? Can you ensure the proper sequence of the seasons, or guide the constellation of the Bear with her satellites across the heavens? Do you know the laws of the universe and how the heavens influence the earth? Can you shout to the clouds and make it rain? Can you make lightning appear and cause it to strike as you direct it? Who gives intuition and instinct? Who is wise enough to number all the clouds? Who can tilt the water jars of heaven, when everything is dust and clods? (Job 38:4–38 TLB)

Promises from Joel

Whoever Calls Shall Be Saved

And it shall come to pass afterward that I will pour out My Spirit on all flesh; your sons and your daughters shall prophesy, your old men shall dream dreams, your young men shall see visions. And also on My menservants and on My maidservants I will pour out My Spirit in those days. And I will show wonders in the heavens and in the earth: Blood and fire and pillars of smoke. The sun shall be turned into darkness, and the moon into blood, before the coming of the great and awesome day of the LORD. And it shall come to pass that whoever calls on the name of the LORD shall be saved. (Joel 2:28–32)

Shall Never Be Put to Shame

Be glad then, you children of Zion, and rejoice in the Lord, your God; for He gives you the former or early rain in just measure and in righteousness, and He causes to come down for you the rain, the former rain and the latter rain, as before....And I will restore or replace for you the years that the locust has eaten—the hopping locust, the stripping locust, and the crawling locust, My great army which I sent among you. And you shall eat in plenty and be satisfied and praise the name of the Lord, your God, Who has dealt wondrously with you. And My people shall never be put to shame. (Joel 2:23, 25–26 AMP)

The Harvest Is Ripe

Put in the sickle, for the harvest is ripe. Come, go down; for the winepress is full, the vats overflow; for their wickedness is great. (Joel 3:13)

Promises from John

Without Him Nothing Was Made

In the beginning was the Word, and the Word was with God, and the Word was God. He was in the beginning with God. All things were made through Him, and without Him nothing was made that was made. (John 1:1–3)

He Created Everything

Before anything else existed, there was Christ, with God. He has always been alive and is himself God. He created everything there is—nothing exists that he didn't make. (John 1:1–3 TLB)

Children of God

But as many as received Him, to them He gave the right to become children of God, to those who believe in His name. (John 1:12)

Word Became Flesh

And the Word became flesh and dwelt among us, and we beheld His glory, the glory as of the only begotten of the Father, full of grace and truth. (John 1:14)

Favor upon Favor

For out of His fullness (abundance) we all received [all had a share and we were all supplied with] one grace after another and spiritual blessing upon spiritual blessing, and even favor upon favor and gift [heaped] upon gift.

(John 1:16 AMP)

Behold the Lamb of God

And John bore witness, saying, "I saw the Spirit descending from heaven like a dove, and He remained upon Him. I did not know Him, but He who sent me to baptize with water said to me, 'Upon whom you see the Spirit descending, and remaining on Him, this is He who baptizes with the Holy Spirit.' And I have seen and testified that this is the Son of God." Again, the next day, John stood with two of his disciples. And looking at Jesus as He walked, he said, "Behold the Lamb of God!" (John 1:32–36)

Angels of God Ascending and Descending

And He said to him, "Most assuredly, I say to you, hereafter you shall see heaven open, and the angels of God ascending and descending upon the Son of Man."

(John 1:51)

You Must Be Born Again

After dark one night a Jewish religious leader named Nicodemus, a member of the sect of the Pharisees, came for an interview with Jesus. "Sir," he said, "we all know that God has sent you to teach us. Your miracles are proof enough of this." Jesus replied, "With all the earnestness I possess I tell you this: Unless you are born again, you can never get into the kingdom of God." "Born again!" exclaimed Nicodemus. "What do you mean? How can an old man go back into his mother's womb and be born again?" Jesus replied, "What I am telling you so earnestly is this: Unless one is born of water and the Spirit, he cannot enter the kingdom of God. Men can only reproduce human life, but the Holy Spirit gives new life from heaven; so don't be surprised at my statement that you must be born again!"
(John 3:1–7 TLB)

Have Eternal Life

So that anyone who believes in me will have eternal life. For God loved the world so much that he gave his only Son so that anyone who believes in him shall not perish but have eternal life.
(John 3:15 TLB)

The World Might Be Saved

For God so loved the world that He gave His only begotten Son, that whoever believes in Him should not perish but have everlasting life. For God did not send His Son into the world to condemn the world, but that the world through Him might be saved.
(John 3:16-17)

He Is above All

He who comes from above is above all; he who is of the earth is earthly and speaks of the earth. He who comes from heaven is above all.
(John 3:31)

Springing Up into Everlasting Life

Jesus answered and said to her, "Whoever drinks of this water will thirst again, but whoever drinks of the water that I shall give him will never thirst. But the water that I shall give him will become in him a fountain of water springing up into everlasting life." (John 4:13–14)

Resurrection of Life

Most assuredly, I say to you, he who hears My word and believes in Him who sent Me has everlasting life, and shall not come into judgment, but has passed from death into life. Most assuredly, I say to you, the hour is coming, and now is, when the dead will hear the voice of the Son of God; and those who hear will live. For as the Father has life in Himself, so He has granted the Son to have life in Himself, and has given Him authority to execute judgment also, because He is the Son of Man. Do not marvel at this; for the hour is coming in which all who are in the graves will hear His voice and come forth; those who have done good, to the resurrection of life, and those who have done evil, to the resurrection of condemnation. (John 5:24–29)

Believe in Him Whom He Sent

"Do not labor for the food which perishes, but for the food which endures to everlasting life, which the Son of Man will give you, because God the Father has set His seal on Him." Then they said to Him, "What shall we do, that we may work the works of God?" Jesus answered and said to them, "This is the work of God, that you believe in Him whom He sent." (John 6:27–29)

Bread from Heaven

Then Jesus said to them, "Most assuredly, I say to you, Moses did not give you the bread from heaven, but My Father gives you the true bread from heaven. For the bread of God is He who comes down from heaven and gives life to the world." Then they said to Him, "Lord, give us this bread always."

(John 6:32–34)

The Bread of Life

And Jesus said to them, "I am the bread of life. He who comes to Me shall never hunger, and he who believes in Me shall never thirst."

(John 6:35)

I Will Raise Him Up at the Last Day

No one can come to Me unless the Father who sent Me draws him; and I will raise him up at the last day.

(John 6:44)

Will Live Forever

Whoever eats My flesh and drinks My blood has eternal life, and I will raise him up at the last day. For My flesh is food indeed, and My blood is drink indeed. He who eats My flesh and drinks My blood abides in Me, and I in him. As the living Father sent Me, and I live because of the Father, so he who feeds on Me will live because of Me. This is the bread which came down from heaven; not as your fathers ate the manna, and are dead. He who eats this bread will live forever.

(John 6:54–58)

They Are Life

It is the Spirit who gives life; the flesh profits nothing. The words that I speak to you are spirit, and they are life. (John 6:63)

The Holy Spirit Gives Eternal Life

Only the Holy Spirit gives eternal life. Those born only once, with physical birth, will never receive this gift. But now I have told you how to get this true spiritual life. (John 6:63 TLB)

Rivers of Living Water

If anyone thirsts, let him come to Me and drink. He who believes in Me, as the Scripture has said, out of his heart will flow rivers of living water. (John 7:37–38)

Light of the World

Then Jesus spoke to them again, saying, "I am the light of the world. He who follows Me shall not walk in darkness, but have the light of life." (John 8:12)

Truth Shall Make You Free

Then Jesus said to those Jews who believed Him, "If you abide in My word, you are My disciples indeed. And you shall know the truth, and the truth shall make you free." (John 8:31–32)

Free Indeed

Therefore if the Son makes you free, you shall be free indeed. (John 8:36)

Keeps My Word

I assure you, most solemnly I tell you, if any one observes My teaching [lives in accordance with My message, keeps My word], he will by no means ever see and experience death.   (John 8:51 AMP)

Shall Never See Death

If anyone keeps My word he shall never see death.   (John 8:52)

I Am the Light of the World

I must work the works of Him who sent Me while it is day; the night is coming when no one can work. As long as I am in the world, I am the light of the world.   (John 9:4–5)

I Am the Door

I am the door. If anyone enters by Me, he will be saved, and will go in and out and find pasture.   (John 10:9)

Life More Abundantly

The thief does not come except to steal, and to kill, and to destroy. I have come that they may have life, and that they may have it more abundantly.   (John 10:10)

I Am the Good Shepherd

I am the good shepherd. The good shepherd gives His life for the sheep.   (John 10:11)

I and My Father Are One

My sheep hear My voice, and I know them, and they follow Me. And I give them eternal life, and they shall never perish; neither shall anyone snatch them out of My hand. My Father, who has given them to Me, is greater than all; and no one is able to snatch them out of My Father's hand. I and My Father are one.

(John 10:27–30)

I Am the Resurrection and the Life

Jesus said to her, "I am the resurrection and the life. He who believes in Me, though he may die, he shall live. And whoever lives and believes in Me shall never die. Do you believe this?"

(John 11:25–26)

See the Glory of God

Jesus said to her, "Did I not say to you that if you would believe you would see the glory of God?"

(John 11:40)

My Father Will Honor

Most assuredly, I say to you, unless a grain of wheat falls into the ground and dies, it remains alone; but if it dies, it produces much grain. He who loves his life will lose it, and he who hates his life in this world will keep it for eternal life. If anyone serves Me, let him follow Me; and where I am, there My servant will be also. If anyone serves Me, him My Father will honor.

(John 12:24–26)

Should Not Abide in Darkness

He who believes in Me, believes not in Me but in Him who sent Me. And he who sees Me sees Him who sent Me. I have come as a light into the world, that whoever believes in Me should not abide in darkness.   (John 12:44–46)

You Are My Disciples

A new commandment I give to you, that you love one another; as I have loved you, that you also love one another. By this all will know that you are My disciples, if you have love for one another.   (John 13:34–35)

Where I Am, There You May Be Also

Let not your heart be troubled; you believe in God, believe also in Me. In My Father's house are many mansions; if it were not so, I would have told you. I go to prepare a place for you. And if I go and prepare a place for you, I will come again and receive you to Myself; that where I am, there you may be also.   (John 14:1–3)

I Am the Way

Jesus said to him, "I am the way, the truth, and the life. No one comes to the Father except through Me."   (John 14:6)

Greater Works than These He Will Do

Believe Me that I am in the Father and the Father in Me, or else believe Me for the sake of the works themselves. Most assuredly, I say to you, he who believes in Me, the works that I do he will do also; and greater works than these he will do, because I go to My Father. And whatever you ask in My name, that I will do, that the Father may be glorified in the Son. If you ask anything in My name, I will do it.   (John 14:11–14)

I Will Love Him

He who has My commandments and keeps them, it is he who loves Me. And he who loves Me will be loved by My Father, and I will love him and manifest Myself to him.   (John 14:21)

Make Our Home with Him

If anyone loves Me, he will keep My word; and My Father will love him, and We will come to him and make Our home with him.   (John 14:23)

Bring to Your Remembrance

But the Helper, the Holy Spirit, whom the Father will send in My name, He will teach you all things, and bring to your remembrance all things that I said to you.   (John 14:26)

But the Comforter (Counselor, Helper, Intercessor, Advocate, Strengthener, Standby), the Holy Spirit, Whom the Father will send in My name [in My place, to represent Me and act on My behalf], He will teach you all things. And He will cause you to recall (will remind you of, bring to your remembrance) everything I have told you.   (John 14:26 AMP)

Neither Let It Be Afraid

Peace I leave with you, My peace I give to you; not as the world gives do I give to you. Let not your heart be troubled, neither let it be afraid.   (John 14:27)

I Am the True Vine

I am the True Vine, and My Father is the Vinedresser. Any branch in Me that does not bear fruit [that stops bearing] He cuts away (trims off, takes away); and He cleanses and repeatedly prunes every branch that continues to bear fruit, to make it bear more and richer and more excellent fruit. You are cleansed and pruned already, because of the word which I have given you [the teachings I have discussed with you]. Dwell in Me, and I will dwell in you. [Live in Me, and I will live in you.] Just as no branch can bear fruit of itself without abiding in (being vitally united to) the vine, neither can you bear fruit unless you abide in Me. I am the Vine; you are the branches. Whoever lives in Me and I in him bears much (abundant) fruit. However, apart from Me [cut off from vital union with Me] you can do nothing....If you live in Me [abide vitally united to Me] and My words remain in you and continue to live in your hearts, ask whatever you will, and it shall be done for you.

(John 15:1–5, 7 AMP)

That Your Joy May Be Full

As the Father loved Me, I also have loved you; abide in My love. If you keep My commandments, you will abide in My love, just as I have kept My Father's commandments and abide in His love. These things I have spoken to you, that My joy may remain in you, and that your joy may be full.

(John 15:9–11)

Keep On Doing

You are My friends if you keep on doing the things which I command you to do.   (John 15:14 AMP)

I Have Chosen You

You have not chosen Me, but I have chosen you and I have appointed you [I have planted you], that you might go and bear fruit and keep on bearing, that your fruit may be lasting [that it may remain, abide], so that whatever you ask the Father in My Name [as presenting all that I AM] He may give it to you.   (John 15:16 AMP)

He Will Guide You into All Truth

Nevertheless I tell you the truth. It is to your advantage that I go away; for if I do not go away, the Helper will not come to you; but if I depart, I will send Him to you. And when He has come, He will convict the world of sin, and of righteousness, and of judgment: of sin, because they do not believe in Me; of righteousness, because I go to My Father and you see Me no more; of judgment, because the ruler of this world is judged. I still have many things to say to you, but you cannot bear them now. However, when He, the Spirit of truth, has come, He will guide you into all truth; for He will not speak on His own authority, but whatever He hears He will speak; and He will tell you things to come.   (John 16:7–13)

That Your Joy May Be Full

Most assuredly, I say to you, whatever you ask the Father in My name He will give you. Until now you have asked nothing in My name. Ask, and you will receive, that your joy may be full.   (John 16:23–24)

I Have Overcome the World

These things I have spoken to you, that in Me you may have peace. In the world you will have tribulation; but be of good cheer, I have overcome the world. (John 16:33)

You Love Them As Much as You Love Me

When Jesus had finished saying all these things he looked up to heaven and said, "Father, the time has come. Reveal the glory of your Son so that he can give the glory back to you. For you have given him authority over every man and woman in all the earth. He gives eternal life to each one you have given him. And this is the way to have eternal life—by knowing you, the only true God, and Jesus Christ, the one you sent to earth! I brought glory to you here on earth by doing everything you told me to. And now, Father, reveal my glory as I stand in your presence, the glory we shared before the world began. I have told these men all about you. They were in the world, but then you gave them to me. Actually, they were always yours, and you gave them to me; and they have obeyed you. Now they know that everything I have is a gift from you, for I have passed on to them the commands you gave me; and they accepted them and know of a certainty that I came down to earth from you, and they believe you sent me. My plea is not for the world but for those you have given me because they belong to you. And all of them, since they are mine, belong to you; and you have given them back to me with everything else of yours, and so they are my glory! Now I am leaving the world, and leaving them behind, and coming to you. Holy Father, keep them in your own care—all those you have given me—so that they will be united just as we are, with none missing. During my time here I have kept safe within your family all of these you gave me. I guarded them so that not one perished, except the son of hell, as the Scriptures foretold. And now I am coming to you. I have told them many things while I was with them so that they would be filled with my joy. I have given them your commands. And the world hates them because they don't fit in with it, just as I don't. I'm not asking you to take them out of the world, but to keep them safe from Satan's power. They are not part of this world any more than I am. Make them pure and holy through teaching them your words of truth. As you sent me into the world, I am sending them into the world, and I consecrate myself to meet their need for growth in truth and holiness. I am not praying for these alone but also for the future believers who will come to me because of the testimony of these. My prayer for all of them is that they will be of one heart and mind, just as you and I are, Father—that just as you are in me and I am in you, so they will be in us, and the world will believe you sent me. I have given them the glory you gave me—the glorious unity of being one, as we are—I in them and you in me, all being perfected into one—so that the world will know you sent me and will understand that you love them as much as you love me. Father, I want them with me—these you've given me—so that they can see my glory. You gave me the glory because you loved me before the world began! O righteous Father, the world doesn't know you, but I do; and these disciples know you sent me. And I have revealed you to them and will keep on revealing you so that the mighty love you have for me may be in them, and I in them.   (John 17:1–26 TLB)

Promises from 1 John

God Is Light

And this is the message [the message of promise] which we have heard from Him and now are reporting to you: God is Light, and there is no darkness in Him at all [no, not in any way].

(1 John 1:5 AMP)

Blood Cleanses Us from All Sin

If we say that we have fellowship with Him, and walk in darkness, we lie and do not practice the truth. But if we walk in the light as He is in the light, we have fellowship with one another, and the blood of Jesus Christ His Son cleanses us from all sin. (1 John 1:6–7)

Cleanse Us from All Unrighteousness

If we confess our sins, He is faithful and just to forgive us our sins and to cleanse us from all unrighteousness. (1 John 1:9)

We Are in Him

But whoever keeps His word, truly the love of God is perfected in him. By this we know that we are in Him. (1 John 2:5)

The True Light Is Always Shining

Again, a new commandment I write to you, which thing is true in Him and in you, because the darkness is passing away, and the true light is already shining. (1 John 2:8)

Abides Forever

He who does the will of God abides forever. (1 John 2:17)

You Know All Things

But you have an anointing from the Holy One, and you know all things. (1 John 2:20)

Eternal Life

If what you heard from the beginning abides in you, you also will abide in the Son and in the Father. And this is the promise that He has promised us; eternal life. (1 John 2:24–25)

You Will Abide in Him

But the anointing which you have received from Him abides in you, and you do not need that anyone teach you; but as the same anointing teaches you concerning all things, and is true, and is not a lie, and just as it has taught you, you will abide in Him. (1 John 2:27)

We Shall See Him

Beloved, now we are children of God; and it has not yet been revealed what we shall be, but we know that when He is revealed, we shall be like Him, for we shall see Him as He is. (1 John 3:2)

He Is Born (Begotten) of God

No one born (begotten) of God [deliberately, knowingly, and habitually] practices sin, for God's nature abides in him [His principle of life, the divine sperm, remains permanently within him]; and he cannot practice sinning because he is born (begotten) of God. (1 John 3:9 AMP)

We Receive from Him

And whatever we ask we receive from Him, because we keep His commandments and do those things that are pleasing in His sight. (1 John 3:22)

Greater than He Who Is in the World

He who is in you is greater than he who is in the world. (1 John 4:4)

Knows God

Beloved, let us love one another, for love is of God; and everyone who loves is born of God and knows God. (1 John 4:7)

We Might Live through Him

In this the love of God was manifested toward us, that God has sent His only begotten Son into the world, that we might live through Him. (1 John 4:9)

Love Perfected in Us

If we love one another, God abides in us, and His love has been perfected in us. (1 John 4:12)

He Has Given Us His Spirit

By this we know that we abide in Him, and He in us, because He has given us of His Spirit. (1 John 4:13)

As He Is, So Are We

Whoever confesses that Jesus is the Son of God, God abides in him, and he in God. And we have known and believed the love that God has for us. God is love, and he who abides in love abides in God, and God in him. Love has been perfected among us in this: that we may have boldness in the day of judgment; because as He is, so are we in this world. (1 John 4:15–17)

Perfect Love Casts Out Fear

There is no fear in love; but perfect love casts out fear. (1 John 4:18 NKJV)

Trusting Christ to Help Him

If you believe that Jesus is the Christ—that he is God's Son and your Savior—then you are a child of God. And all who love the Father love his children too. So you can find out how much you love God's children—your brothers and sisters in the Lord—by how much you love and obey God. Loving God means doing what he tells us to do, and really, that isn't hard at all; for every child of God can obey him, defeating sin and evil pleasure by trusting Christ to help him. (1 John 5:1–4 TLB)

He Will Answer Us

So whoever has God's Son has life; whoever does not have his Son, does not have life. I have written this to you who believe in the Son of God so that you may know you have eternal life. And we are sure of this, that he will listen to us whenever we ask him for anything in line with his will. And if we really know he is listening when we talk to him and make our requests, then we can be sure that he will answer us. (1 John 5:12–15 TLB)

Promises from 2 John

Much Peace, Truth, and Love

Since the Truth is in our hearts forever, God the Father and Jesus Christ his Son will bless us with great mercy and much peace, and with truth and love. (2 John 2–3 TLB)

Promises from 3 John

Your Soul Prospers

Beloved, I pray that you may prosper in all things and be in health, just as your soul prospers.

(3 John 2)

Children Walk in Truth

I have no greater joy than to hear that my children walk in truth.

(3 John 4)

Is of God

He who does good is of God, but he who does evil has not seen God.

(3 John 11)

Promises from Jonah

Abundant in Lovingkindness

You are a gracious and merciful God, slow to anger and abundant in lovingkindness, One who relents from doing harm.

(Jonah 4:2)

You Revoke Evil against Them

You are a gracious God and merciful, slow to anger and of great kindness, and [when sinners turn to You and meet Your conditions] You revoke the [sentence of] evil against them.　　(Jonah 4:2 AMP)

Promises from Joshua

I Have Given You

Every place that the sole of your foot will tread upon I have given you, as I said to Moses.　　(Joshua 1:3)

Will Not Forsake You

I will not leave you nor forsake you.　　(Joshua 1:5)

God Is with You

Have I not commanded you? Be strong and of good courage; do not be afraid, nor be dismayed, for the LORD your God is with you wherever you go.　　(Joshua 1:9)

God Is Giving You Rest

The LORD your God is giving you rest and is giving you this land.　　(Joshua 1:13)

God Be with You

The LORD your God be with you, as He was with Moses. (Joshua 1:17)

The Hand of the Lord Is Mighty

You shall let your children know, Israel came over this Jordan on dry ground. For the Lord your God dried up the waters of the Jordan for you until you passed over, as the Lord your God did to the Red Sea, which He dried up for us until we passed over, that all the peoples of the earth may know that the hand of the Lord is mighty and that you may reverence and fear the Lord your God forever. (Joshua 4:22–24 AMP)

It Is the Lord Who Fights for You

One man of you shall put to flight a thousand, for it is the Lord your God Who fights for you, as He promised you. (Joshua 23:10 AMP)

Not One Word Has Failed

Not one thing has failed of all the good things which the LORD your God spoke concerning you. All have come to pass for you; and not one word of them has failed. (Joshua 23:14)

Promises from Joshua

Promises from Jude

Rise like an Edifice Higher and Higher

But you, beloved, build yourselves up [founded] on your most holy faith [make progress, rise like an edifice higher and higher], praying in the Holy Spirit. (Jude 20 AMP)

Keep You without Stumbling

Now to Him who is able to keep you from stumbling, and to present you faultless before the presence of His glory with exceeding joy, to God our Savior, who alone is wise, be glory and majesty, dominion and power, both now and forever. Amen. (Jude 24–25)

Now to Him Who is able to keep you without stumbling or slipping or falling, and to present [you] unblemished (blameless and faultless) before the presence of His glory in triumphant joy and exultation [with unspeakable, ecstatic delight]—to the one only God, our Savior through Jesus Christ our Lord, be glory (splendor), majesty, might and dominion, and power and authority, before all time and now and forever (unto all the ages of eternity). Amen (so be it). (Jude 24–25 AMP)

Promises from Judges

Never Break

I said, "I will never break My covenant with you." (Judges 2:1)

I Am

I am the LORD your God.

(Judges 6:10)

You Shall Not Die

Peace be with you; do not fear, you shall not die.

(Judges 6:23)

You Shall Conceive

And the Angel of the LORD appeared to the woman and said to her, "Indeed now, you are barren and have borne no children, but you shall conceive and bear a son."

(Judges 13:3)

Promises from I Kings

I Have a Wise and Understanding Heart

"Therefore give to Your servant an understanding heart to judge Your people, that I may discern between good and evil. For who is able to judge this great people of Yours?" The speech pleased the LORD, that Solomon had asked this thing. Then God said to him: "Because you have asked this thing, and have not asked long life for yourself, nor have asked riches for yourself, nor have asked the life of your enemies, but have asked for yourself understanding to discern justice, behold, I have done according to your words; see, I have given you a wise and understanding heart, so that there has not been anyone like you before you, nor shall any like you arise after you. And I have also given you what you have not asked: both riches and honor, so that there shall not be anyone like you among the kings all your days."

(1 Kings 3:9–13)

There Has Not Failed One Word

There has not failed one word of all His good promise. (1 Kings 8:56)

Nor Shall the Jar of Oil Run Dry

So she said, "As the Lord your God lives, I do not have bread, only a handful of flour in a bin, and a little oil in a jar; and see, I am gathering a couple of sticks that I may go in and prepare it for myself and my son, that we may eat it, and die." And Elijah said to her, "Do not fear; go and do as you have said, but make me a small cake from it first, and bring it to me; and afterward make some for yourself and your son. For thus says the Lord God of Israel: 'The bin of flour shall not be used up, nor shall the jar of oil run dry, until the day the Lord sends rain on the earth.'" So she went away and did according to the word of Elijah; and she and he and her household ate for many days. The bin of flour was not used up, nor did the jar of oil run dry, according to the word of the Lord which He spoke by Elijah. (1 Kings 17:12–16)

Promises from 2 Kings

He Prospered Wherever He Went

For he held fast to the Lord; he did not depart from following Him, but kept His commandments, which the Lord had commanded Moses. The Lord was with him; he prospered wherever he went. (2 Kings 18:6–7)

Surely I Will Heal You

I have heard your prayer, I have seen your tears; surely I will heal you. (2 Kings 20:5)

Promises from Lamentations

The Lord Is Righteous

The Lord is righteous (just and in the right). (Lamentations 1:18 AMP)

New Every Morning

Through the Lord's mercies we are not consumed, because His compassions fail not. They are new every morning; great is Your faithfulness. "The LORD is my portion," says my soul, "therefore I hope in Him!" The LORD is good to those who wait for Him, to the soul who seeks Him. (Lamentations 3:22–25)

Do Not Fear

I called on Your name, O LORD, from the lowest pit. You have heard my voice: "Do not hide Your ear from my sighing, from my cry for help." You drew near on the day I called on You, and said, "Do not fear!" (Lamentations 3:55–57)

From Generation to Generation

You, O LORD, remain forever; your throne from generation to generation. (Lamentations 5:19)

Promises from Leviticus

The Glory of the Lord

And all the congregation drew near and stood before the LORD. Then Moses said, "This is the thing which the LORD commanded you to do, and the glory of the LORD will appear to you."

(Leviticus 9:5–6)

I Am Holy

For I am the LORD your God. You shall therefore consecrate yourselves, and you shall be holy; for I am holy.

(Leviticus 11:44)

I Am

I am the LORD your God.

(Leviticus 18:4)

I the Lord Your God Am Holy

You shall be holy, for I the LORD your God am holy.

(Leviticus 19:2)

You Should Be Mine

And you shall be holy to Me, for I the LORD am holy, and have separated you from the peoples, that you should be Mine.

(Leviticus 20:26)

I Am the Lord Your God

Therefore you shall not oppress one another, but you shall fear your God; for I am the LORD your God. (Leviticus 25:17)

I Will Be Your God

You shall keep My Sabbaths and reverence My sanctuary: I am the LORD. If you walk in My statutes and keep My commandments, and perform them, then I will give you rain in its season, the land shall yield its produce, and the trees of the field shall yield their fruit. Your threshing shall last till the time of vintage, and the vintage shall last till the time of sowing; you shall eat your bread to the full, and dwell in your land safely. I will give peace in the land, and you shall lie down, and none will make you afraid; I will rid the land of evil beasts, and the sword will not go through your land. You will chase your enemies, and they shall fall by the sword before you. Five of you shall chase a hundred, and a hundred of you shall put ten thousand to flight; your enemies shall fall by the sword before you. For I will look on you favorably and make you fruitful, multiply you and confirm My covenant with you. You shall eat the old harvest, and clear out the old because of the new. I will set My tabernacle among you, and My soul shall not abhor you. I will walk among you and be your God, and you shall be My people. I am the LORD your God, who brought you out of the land of Egypt, that you should not be their slaves; I have broken the bands of your yoke and made you walk upright. (Leviticus 26:2–13)

It Is Holy to the Lord

And all the tithe of the land whether of the seed of the land or of the fruit of the tree, is the Lord's. It is holy to the LORD. (Leviticus 27:30)

Promises from Luke

With God Nothing Will Be Impossible

And the angel answered and said to her, "The Holy Spirit will come upon you, and the power of the Highest will overshadow you; therefore, also, that Holy One who is to be born will be called the Son of God. Now indeed, Elizabeth your relative has also conceived a son in her old age; and this is now the sixth month for her who was called barren. For with God nothing will be impossible."

(Luke 1:35–37)

No Word from God Shall Be without Power

For with God nothing is ever impossible and no word from God shall be without power or impossible of fulfillment.

(Luke 1:37 AMP)

Every Promise Shall Come True

For every promise from God shall surely come true.

(Luke 1:37 TLB)

Straight Line into the Way of Peace

A Light from on high will dawn upon us and visit [us] to shine upon and give light to those who sit in darkness and in the shadow of death, to direct and guide our feet in a straight line into the way of peace.

(Luke 1:78–79 AMP)

A Savior, Who Is Christ the Lord

And behold, an angel of the Lord stood before them, and the glory of the Lord shone around them, and they were greatly afraid. Then the angel said to them, "Do not be afraid, for behold, I bring you good tidings of great joy which will be to all people. For there is born to you this day in the city of David a Savior, who is Christ the Lord."
(Luke 2:9–11)

The Most Joyful News Ever Announced

Suddenly an angel appeared among them, and the landscape shone bright with the glory of the Lord. They were badly frightened, but the angel reassured them. "Don't be afraid!" he said. "I bring you the most joyful news ever announced, and it is for everyone! The Savior—yes, the Messiah, the Lord—has been born tonight in Bethlehem!"
(Luke 2:9–11 TLB)

Deliverance from Eternal Death

Every valley and ravine shall be filled up, and every mountain and hill shall be leveled; and the crooked places shall be made straight, and the rough roads shall be made smooth; and all mankind shall see (behold and understand and at last acknowledge) the salvation of God (the deliverance from eternal death decreed by God).
(Luke 3:5–6 AMP)

Children from Stones

For I say to you that God is able to raise up children to Abraham from these stones.
(Luke 3:8)

Baptize with Holy Spirit and Fire

John answered, saying to all, "I indeed baptize you with water; but One mightier than I is coming, whose sandal strap I am not worthy to loose. He will baptize you with the Holy Spirit and fire."

(Luke 3:16)

Every Word of God

But Jesus answered him, saying, "It is written, 'Man shall not live by bread alone, but by every word of God.'"

(Luke 4:4)

Today Scripture Is Fulfilled

"The Spirit of the LORD is upon Me, because He has anointed Me to preach the gospel to the poor; He has sent Me to heal the brokenhearted, to proclaim liberty to the captives and recovery of sight to the blind, to set at liberty those who are oppressed; to proclaim the acceptable year of the LORD." Then He closed the book, and gave it back to the attendant and sat down. And the eyes of all who were in the synagogue were fixed on Him. And He began to say to them, "Today this Scripture is fulfilled in your hearing."

(Luke 4:18–21)

Your Reward Will Be Great

But love your enemies and be kind and do good [doing favors so that someone derives benefit from them] and lend, expecting and hoping for nothing in return but considering nothing as lost and despairing of no one; and then your recompense (your reward) will be great (rich, strong, intense, and abundant), and you will be sons of the Most High, for He is kind and charitable and good to the ungrateful and the selfish and wicked. So be merciful (sympathetic, tender, responsive, and compassionate) even as your Father is [all these].

(Luke 6:35–36 AMP)

Will Be Given Back to You

For if you give, you will get! Your gift will return to you in full and overflowing measure, pressed down, shaken together to make room for more, and running over. Whatever measure you use to give—large or small—will be used to measure what is given back to you.   (Luke 6:38 TLB)

Produces What Is Upright

The upright (honorable, intrinsically good) man out of the good treasure [stored] in his heart produces what is upright (honorable and intrinsically good).   (Luke 6:45 AMP)

The Dead Are Raised Up

And that very hour He cured many of infirmities, afflictions, and evil spirits; and to many blind He gave sight. Jesus answered and said to them, "Go and tell John the things you have seen and heard: that the blind see, the lame walk, the lepers are cleansed, the deaf hear, the dead are raised, the poor have the gospel preached to them. And blessed is he who is not offended because of Me."   (Luke 7:21–23)

Does Not Lose His Faith in Me

And tell him, "Blessed is the one who does not lose his faith in me."   (Luke 7:23 TLB)

More Will Be Given

No one, when he has lit a lamp, covers it with a vessel or puts it under a bed, but sets it on a lampstand, that those who enter may see the light. For nothing is secret that will not be revealed, nor anything hidden that will not be known and come to light. Therefore take heed how you hear. For whoever has, to him more will be given; and whoever does not have, even what he seems to have will be taken from him.

(Luke 8:16–18)

Do It

But He answered and said to them, "My mother and My brothers are these who hear the word of God and do it."

(Luke 8:21)

Your Faith Has Made You Well

And a woman who had suffered from a flow of blood for twelve years and had spent all her living upon physicians, and could not be healed by anyone, came up behind Him and touched the fringe of His garment, and immediately her flow of blood ceased. And Jesus said, Who is it who touched Me? When all were denying it, Peter and those who were with him said, Master, the multitudes surround You and press You on every side! But Jesus said, Someone did touch Me; for I perceived that [healing] power has gone forth from Me. And when the woman saw that she had not escaped notice, she came up trembling, and, falling down before Him, she declared in the presence of all the people for what reason she had touched Him and how she had been instantly cured. And He said to her, Daughter, your faith (your confidence and trust in Me) has made you well! Go (enter) into peace (untroubled, undisturbed well-being).

(Luke 8:43–48 AMP)

Only Believe

But when Jesus heard it, He answered him, saying, "Do not be afraid; only believe, and she will be made well." (Luke 8:50)

Power and Authority

Then He called His twelve disciples together and gave them power and authority over all demons, and to cure diseases. He sent them to preach the kingdom of God and to heal the sick. (Luke 9:1–2)

He Will Preserve and Save It

Then He said to them all, "If anyone desires to come after Me, let him deny himself, and take up his cross daily, and follow Me. For whoever desires to save his life will lose it, but whoever loses his life for My sake will save it." (Luke 9:23–24)

The Measure of Your Greatness

[Jesus] said to them, "Anyone who takes care of a little child like this is caring for me! And whoever cares for me is caring for God who sent me. Your care for others is the measure of your greatness." (Luke 9:48 TLB)

Save From Penalty of Eternal Death

For the Son of man did not come to destroy men's lives, but to save them [from the penalty of eternal death]. (Luke 9:56 AMP)

Your Names Are Written in Heaven

Behold, I give you the authority to trample on serpents and scorpions, and over all the power of the enemy, and nothing shall by any means hurt you. Nevertheless do not rejoice in this, that the spirits are subject to you, but rather rejoice because your names are written in heaven.   (Luke 10:19–20)

Do This and You Will Live

And behold, a certain lawyer stood up and tested Him, saying, "Teacher, what shall I do to inherit eternal life?" He said to him, "What is written in the law? What is your reading of it?" So he answered and said, "'You shall love the LORD your God with all your heart, with all your soul, with all your strength, and with all your mind,' and 'your neighbor as yourself.'" And He said to him, "You have answered rightly; do this and you will live."   (Luke 10:25–28)

The Door Shall Be Opened

So I say to you, Ask and keep on asking and it shall be given you; seek and keep on seeking and you shall find; knock and keep on knocking and the door shall be opened to you. For everyone who asks and keeps on asking receives; and he who seeks and keeps on seeking finds; and to him who knocks and keeps on knocking, the door shall be opened.   (Luke 11:9–10 AMP)

Give the Holy Spirit

If you then, evil as you are, know how to give good gifts [gifts that are to their advantage] to your children, how much more will your heavenly Father give the Holy Spirit to those who ask and continue to ask Him!   (Luke 11:13 AMP)

Keep It

But He said, "More than that, blessed are those who hear the word of God and keep it!" (Luke 11:28)

Put It into Practice

He replied, "Yes, but even more blessed are all who hear the Word of God and put it into practice."
(Luke 11:28 TLB)

Your Face Will Be Radiant, Too

No one lights a lamp and hides it! Instead, he puts it on a lampstand to give light to all who enter the room. Your eyes light up your inward being. A pure eye lets sunshine into your soul. A lustful eye shuts out the light and plunges you into darkness. So watch out that the sunshine isn't blotted out. If you are filled with light within, with no dark corners, then your face will be radiant too, as though a floodlight is beamed upon you. (Luke 11:33–36 TLB)

Acknowledge before the Angels

And I tell you, Whoever declares openly [speaking out freely] and confesses that he is My worshiper and acknowledges Me before men, the Son of Man also will declare and confess and acknowledge him before the angels of God. (Luke 12:8 AMP)

What to Say

Do not be anxious [beforehand] how you shall reply in defense or what you are to say. For the Holy Spirit will teach you in that very hour and moment what [you] ought to say. (Luke 12:11–12 AMP)

He Will Always Give You All You Need

Then turning to his disciples he said, "Don't worry about whether you have enough food to eat or clothes to wear. For life consists of far more than food and clothes. Look at the ravens—they don't plant or harvest or have barns to store away their food, and yet they get along all right—for God feeds them. And you are far more valuable to him than any birds! And besides, what's the use of worrying? What good does it do? Will it add a single day to your life? Of course not! And if worry can't even do such little things as that, what's the use of worrying over bigger things? Look at the lilies! They don't toil and spin, and yet Solomon in all his glory was not robed as well as they are. And if God provides clothing for the flowers that are here today and gone tomorrow, don't you suppose that he will provide clothing for you, you doubters? And don't worry about food—what to eat and drink; don't worry at all that God will provide it for you. All mankind scratches for its daily bread, but your heavenly Father knows your needs. He will always give you all you need from day to day if you will make the kingdom of God your primary concern. So don't be afraid, little flock. For it gives your Father great happiness to give you the kingdom." (Luke 12:22–32 TLB)

No Thief Can Steal Them

Sell what you have and give to those in need. This will fatten your purses in heaven! And the purses of heaven have no rips or holes in them. Your treasures there will never disappear; no thief can steal them; no moth can destroy them. Wherever your treasure is, there your heart and thoughts will also be. (Luke 12:33–34 TLB)

More Joy in Heaven

Thus, I tell you, there will be more joy in heaven over one [especially] wicked person who repents (changes his mind, abhorring his errors and misdeeds, and determines to enter upon a better course of life) than over ninety-nine righteous persons who have no need of repentance. (Luke 15:7 AMP)

It Would Obey You

And the apostles said to the Lord, "Increase our faith." So the Lord said, "If you have faith as a mustard seed, you can say to this mulberry tree, 'Be pulled up by the roots and be planted in the sea,' and it would obey you."   (Luke 17:5–6)

Will Be in His Day

For as the lightning that flashes out of one part under heaven shines to the other part under heaven, so also the Son of Man will be in His day.   (Luke 17:24)

Will Preserve It

Whoever seeks to save his life will lose it, and whoever loses his life will preserve it.   (Luke 17:33)

Such Is the Kingdom of God

But Jesus called them to Him and said, "Let the little children come to Me, and do not forbid them; for of such is the kingdom of God."   (Luke 18:16)

Possible with God

But He said, "The things which are impossible with men are possible with God."   (Luke 18:27)

Eternal Life

Assuredly, I say to you, there is no one who has left house or parents or brothers or wife or children, for the sake of the kingdom of God, who shall not receive many times more in this present time, and in the age to come eternal life.

(Luke 18:29–30)

Save That Which Was Lost

For the Son of Man has come to seek and to save that which was lost.

(Luke 19:10)

Your Redemption Draws Near

And there will be signs in the sun, in the moon, and in the stars; and on the earth distress of nations, with perplexity, the sea and the waves roaring; men's hearts failing them from fear and the expectation of those things which are coming on the earth, for the powers of heaven will be shaken. Then they will see the Son of Man coming in a cloud with power and great glory. Now when these things begin to happen, look up and lift up your heads, because your redemption draws near.

(Luke 21:25–28)

Forever True

And though all heaven and earth shall pass away, yet my words remain forever true.

(Luke 21:33 TLB)

New Covenant

And He took bread, gave thanks and broke it, and gave it to them, saying, "This is My body which is given for you; do this in remembrance of Me." Likewise He also took the cup after supper, saying, "This cup is the new covenant in My blood, which is shed for you." (Luke 22:19–20)

Sit on the Right Hand

Hereafter the Son of Man will sit on the right hand of the power of God. (Luke 22:69)

Carried Up into Heaven

Now it came to pass, while He blessed them, that He was parted from them and carried up into heaven. (Luke 24:51)

Promises from Malachi

My Name Shall Be Great

"For from the rising of the sun, even to its going down, My name shall be great among the Gentiles; in every place incense shall be offered to My name, and a pure offering; for My name shall be great among the nations," says the LORD of hosts. (Malachi 1:11)

My Name Is to Be Feared

"For I am a great King," says the LORD of hosts, "and My name is to be feared among the nations."

(Malachi 1:14)

I Do Not Change

For I am the LORD, I do not change.

(Malachi 3:6)

I Will Return to You

"Return to Me, and I will return to you," says the LORD of hosts.

(Malachi 3:7)

Try Me Now

"Bring all the tithes into the storehouse, that there may be food in My house, and try Me now in this," says the LORD of hosts, "if I will not open for you the windows of heaven and pour out for you such blessing that there will not be room enough to receive it."

(Malachi 3:10)

You Will Be a Delightful Land

"And I will rebuke the devourer for your sakes, so that he will not destory the fruit of your ground, nor shall the vine fail to bear fruit for you in the field," says the LORD of hosts; "and all nations will call you blessed, for you will be a delightful land," says the LORD of hosts.

(Malachi 3:11–12)

Make Them My Jewels

"They shall be Mine," says the LORD of hosts, "on the day that I make them My jewels. And I will spare them as a man spares his own son who serves him." Then you shall again discern between the righteous and the wicked, between one who serves God and one who does not serve Him.

(Malachi 3:17–18)

Leap for Joy

But unto you who revere and worshipfully fear My name shall the Sun of Righteousness arise with healing in His wings and His beams, and you shall go forth and gambol like calves [released] from the stall and leap for joy.

(Malachi 4:2 AMP)

Promises from Mark

So That God Could Forgive Them

Here begins the wonderful story of Jesus the Messiah, the Son of God. In the book written by the prophet Isaiah, God announced that he would send his Son to earth, and that a special messenger would arrive first to prepare the world for his coming. "This messenger will live out in the barren wilderness," Isaiah said, "and will proclaim that everyone must straighten out his life to be ready for the Lord's arrival." This messenger was John the Baptist. He lived in the wilderness and taught that all should be baptized as a public announcement of their decision to turn their backs on sin, so that God could forgive them.

(Mark 1:1–4 TLB)

Baptize You with the Holy Spirit

And he preached, saying, After me comes He Who is stronger (more powerful and more valiant) than I, the strap of Whose sandals I am not worthy or fit to stoop down and unloose. I have baptized you with water, but He will baptize you with the Holy Spirit. (Mark 1:7–8 AMP)

Fishers of Men

Then Jesus said to them, "Follow Me, and I will make you become fishers of men." (Mark 1:17)

Fishermen for the Souls of Men

Jesus called out to them, "Come, follow me! And I will make you fishermen for the souls of men!" (Mark 1:17 TLB)

Sinners to Repentance

Those who are well have no need of a physician, but those who are sick. I did not come to call the righteous, but sinners, to repentance. (Mark 2:17)

Lord of the Sabbath

The Sabbath was made for man, and not man for the Sabbath. Therefore the Son of Man is also Lord of the Sabbath. (Mark 2:27–28)

Will of God

For whoever does the will of God is My brother and My sister and mother. (Mark 3:35)

Some a Hundred

But these are the ones sown on good ground, those who hear the word, accept it, and bear fruit: some thirtyfold, some sixty, and some a hundred. (Mark 4:20)

Come to Light

For there is nothing hidden which will not be revealed, nor has anything been kept secret but that it should come to light. (Mark 4:22)

More Will Be Given

And He said to them, Be careful what you are hearing. The measure [of thought and study] you give [to the truth you hear] will be the measure [of virtue and knowledge] that comes back to you—and more [besides] will be given to you who hear. (Mark 4:24 AMP)

Free from Your Disease

And He said to her, Daughter, your faith (your trust and confidence in Me, springing from faith in God) has restored you to health. Go in (into) peace and be continually healed and freed from your [distressing bodily] disease. (Mark 5:34 AMP)

Made Well

Wherever He entered into villages, cities, or in the country, they laid the sick in the marketplaces, and begged Him that they might just touch the hem of His garment. And as many as touched Him were made well. (Mark 6:56)

Eternal Kingdom

For whoever wants to save his [higher, spiritual, eternal] life, will lose it [the lower, natural, temporal life which is lived only on earth]; and whoever gives up his life [which is lived only on earth] for My sake and the Gospel's will save it [his higher, spiritual life in the eternal kingdom of God].

(Mark 8:35 AMP)

All Things Are Possible

Jesus said to him, "If you can believe, all things are possible to him who believes."

(Mark 9:23)

Servant of All

And He sat down, called the twelve, and said to them, "If anyone desires to be first, he shall be last of all and servant of all."

(Mark 9:35)

Two Shall Become One Flesh

But from the beginning of the creation, God "made them male and female." "For this reason a man shall leave his father and mother and be joined to his wife, and the two shall become one flesh"; so then they are no longer two, but one flesh. Therefore what God has joined together, let not man separate.

(Mark 10:6–9)

All Things Are Possible with God

But Jesus looked at them and said, "With men it is impossible, but not with God; for with God all things are possible."

(Mark 10:27)

Hundredfold Now

So Jesus answered and said, "Assuredly, I say to you, there is no one who has left house or brothers or sisters or father or mother or wife or children or lands, for My sake and the gospel's, who shall not receive a hundredfold now in this time; houses and brothers and sisters and mothers and children and lands, with persecutions; and in the age to come, eternal life." (Mark 10:29–30)

Faith Has Made You Well

Then many warned him to be quiet; but he cried out all the more, "Son of David, have mercy on me!" Then Jesus said to him, "Go your way; your faith has made you well." And immediately he received his sight and followed Jesus on the road. (Mark 10:48, 52)

Who Comes in the Name of the Lord

Then those who went before and those who followed cried out, saying: "Hosanna! 'Blessed is He who comes in the name of the Lord!'" (Mark 11:9)

You Will Have Them

So Jesus answered and said to them, "Have faith in God. For assuredly, I say to you, whoever says to this mountain, 'Be removed and be cast into the sea,' and does not doubt in his heart, but believes that those things he says will be done, he will have whatever he says. Therefore I say to you, whatever things you ask when you pray, believe that you receive them, and you will have them. And whenever you stand praying, if you have anything against anyone, forgive him, that your Father in heaven may also forgive you your trespasses. But if you do not forgive, neither will your Father in heaven forgive your trespasses." (Mark 11:22–26)

If You Believe, It's Yours

In reply Jesus said to the disciples, "If you only have faith in God—this is the absolute truth—you can say to this Mount of Olives, 'Rise up and fall into the Mediterranean,' and your command will be obeyed. All that's required is that you really believe and have no doubt! Listen to me! You can pray for anything, and if you believe, you have it; it's yours!" (Mark 11:22–24 TLB)

You Will Get It

For this reason I am telling you, whatever you ask for in prayer, believe (trust and be confident) that it is granted to you, and you will [get it]. (Mark 11:24 AMP)

They Will Recover

And He said to them, "Go into all the world and preach the gospel to every creature. He who believes and is baptized will be saved; but he who does not believe will be condemned. And these signs will follow those who believe: In My name they will cast out demons; they will speak with new tongues; they will take up serpents; and if they drink anything deadly, it will by no means hurt them; they will lay hands on the sick, and they will recover." (Mark 16:15–18)

Promises from Matthew

Mother of Jesus Christ

Jacob was the father of Joseph (who was the husband of Mary, the mother of Jesus Christ the Messiah). (Matthew 1:16 TLB)

He Will Save His People

But while he thought about these things, behold, an angel of the Lord appeared to him in a dream, saying, "Joseph, son of David, do not be afraid to take to you Mary your wife, for that which is conceived in her is of the Holy Spirit. And she will bring forth a Son, and you shall call His name JESUS, for He will save His people from their sins." (Matthew 1:20–21)

God with Us

"Behold, the virgin shall be with child, and bear a Son, and they shall call His name Immanuel," which is translated, "God with us." (Matthew 1:23)

Joseph Named Him Jesus

When Joseph awoke, he did as the angel commanded, and brought Mary home to be his wife, but she remained a virgin until her Son was born; and Joseph named him "Jesus." (Matthew 1:24–25 TLB)

Star Stood Over

When they heard the king, they departed; and behold, the star which they had seen in the East went before them, till it came and stood over where the young Child was. (Matthew 2:9)

Baptize You with the Holy Spirit

I indeed baptize you with water unto repentance, but He who is coming after me is mightier than I, whose sandals I am not worthy to carry. He will baptize you with the Holy Spirit and fire. (Matthew 3:11)

I Am Well Pleased

When He had been baptized, Jesus came up immediately from the water; and behold, the heavens were opened to Him, and He saw the Spirit of God descending like a dove and alighting upon Him. And suddenly a voice came from heaven, saying, "This is My beloved Son, in whom I am well pleased."

(Matthew 3:16–17)

Every Word

But He answered and said, "It is written, 'Man shall not live by bread alone, but by every word that proceeds from the mouth of God.'"

(Matthew 4:4)

But He replied, It has been written, Man shall not live and be upheld and sustained by bread alone, but by every word that comes forth from the mouth of God.

(Matthew 4:4 AMP)

I Will Make You

Then He said to them, "Follow Me, and I will make you fishers of men."

(Matthew 4:19)

He Healed Them All

Then His fame went throughout all Syria; and they brought to Him all sick people who were afflicted with various diseases and torments, and those who were demon-possessed, epileptics, and paralytics; and He healed them.

(Matthew 4:24)

The report of his miracles spread far beyond the borders of Galilee so that sick folk were soon coming to be healed from as far away as Syria. And whatever their illness and pain, or if they were possessed by demons, or were insane, or paralyzed—he healed them all.

(Matthew 4:24 TLB)

Theirs Is the Kingdom of Heaven

Blessed are the poor in spirit, for theirs is the kingdom of heaven. Blessed are those who mourn, for they shall be comforted. Blessed are the meek, for they shall inherit the earth. Blessed are those who hunger and thirst for righteousness, for they shall be filled. Blessed are the merciful, for they shall obtain mercy. Blessed are the pure in heart, for they shall see God. Blessed are the peacemakers, for they shall be called sons of God. Blessed are those who are persecuted for righteousness' sake, for theirs is the kingdom of heaven.   (Matthew 5:3–10)

Strong and Intense

Be glad and supremely joyful, for your reward in heaven is great (strong and intense), for in this same way people persecuted the prophets who were before you.   (Matthew 5:12 AMP)

Salt

You are the salt of the earth; but if the salt loses its flavor, how shall it be seasoned? It is then good for nothing but to be thrown out and trampled underfoot by men.   (Matthew 5:13)

Light of the World

You are the light of the world. A city that is set on a hill cannot be hidden. Nor do they light a lamp and put it under a basket, but on a lampstand, and it gives light to all who are in the house. Let your light so shine before men, that they may see your good works and glorify your Father in heaven. (Matthew 5:14–16)

Purpose Is Achieved

With all the earnestness I have I say: Every law in the Book will continue until its purpose is achieved.   (Matthew 5:18 TLB)

Great in the Kingdom of Heaven

Whoever therefore breaks one of the least of these commandments, and teaches men so, shall be called least in the kingdom of heaven; but whoever does and teaches them, he shall be called great in the kingdom of heaven.   (Matthew 5:19)

Father in Heaven Is Perfect

Therefore you shall be perfect, just as your Father in heaven is perfect.   (Matthew 5:48)

Virtue and Integrity

You, therefore, must be perfect [growing into complete maturity of godliness in mind and character, having reached the proper height of virtue and integrity], as your heavenly Father is perfect.   (Matthew 5:48 AMP)

Heavenly Father Will Also Forgive You

In this manner, therefore, pray: Our Father in heaven, hallowed be Your name. Your kingdom come. Your will be done on earth as it is in heaven. Give us this day our daily bread. And forgive us our debts, as we forgive our debtors. And do not lead us into temptation, but deliver us from the evil one. For Yours is the kingdom and the power and the glory forever. Amen. For if you forgive men their trespasses, your heavenly Father will also forgive you.   (Matthew 6:9–14)

Treasures in Heaven

Do not lay up for yourselves treasures on earth, where moth and rust destroy and where thieves break in and steal; but lay up for yourselves treasures in heaven, where neither moth nor rust destroys and where thieves do not break in and steal. (Matthew 6:19–20)

These Things Shall Be Added to You

Do not worry about your life, what you will eat or what you will drink; nor about your body, what you will put on. Is not life more than food and the body more than clothing? Look at the birds of the air, for they neither sow nor reap nor gather into barns; yet your heavenly Father feeds them. Are you not of more value than they? Which of you by worrying can add one cubit to his stature? So why do you worry about clothing? Consider the lilies of the field, how they grow: they neither toil nor spin; and yet I say to you that even Solomon in all his glory was not arrayed like one of these. Now if God so clothes the grass of the field, which today is, and tomorrow is thrown into the oven, will He not much more clothe you, O you of little faith? Therefore do not worry, saying, "What shall we eat?" or "What shall we drink?" or "What shall we wear?" For after all these things the Gentiles seek. For your heavenly Father knows that you need all these things. But seek first the kingdom of God and His righteousness, and all these things shall be added to you. (Matthew 6:25–33)

Ask, Seek, Knock

Ask, and it will be given to you; seek, and you will find; knock, and it will be opened to you. For everyone who asks receives, and he who seeks finds, and to him who knocks it will be opened. (Matthew 7:7–8)

Father Gives Good Things

Or what man is there among you who, if his son asks for bread, will give him a stone? Or if he asks for a fish, will he give him a serpent? If you then, being evil, know how to give good gifts to your children, how much more will your Father who is in heaven give good things to those who ask Him!

(Matthew 7:9–11)

He Who Does the Will of My Father

Not everyone who says to Me, "Lord, Lord," shall enter the kingdom of heaven, but he who does the will of My Father in heaven.

(Matthew 7:21)

It Was Founded on the Rock

Therefore whoever hears these sayings of Mine, and does them, I will liken him to a wise man who built his house on the rock: and the rain descended, the floods came, and the winds blew and beat on that house; and it did not fall, for it was founded on the rock.

(Matthew 7:24–25)

I Am Willing

When He had come down from the mountain, great multitudes followed Him. And behold, a leper came and worshiped Him, saying, "Lord, if You are willing, You can make me clean." Then Jesus put out His hand and touched him, saying, "I am willing; be cleansed." Immediately his leprosy was cleansed.

(Matthew 8:1–3)

Healed That Same Hour

"As you have believed, so let it be done for you." And his servant was healed that same hour.

(Matthew 8:13)

Fever Left

Now when Jesus had come into Peter's house, He saw his wife's mother lying sick with a fever. So He touched her hand, and the fever left her. And she arose and served them. (Matthew 8:14–15)

Healed All Who Were Sick

When evening had come, they brought to Him many who were demon-possessed. And He cast out the spirits with a word, and healed all who were sick. (Matthew 8:16)

Bore Our Sicknesses

He Himself took our infirmities and bore our sicknesses. (Matthew 8:17)

Both Are Preserved

No one puts a piece of unshrunk cloth on an old garment; for the patch pulls away from the garment, and the tear is made worse. Nor do they put new wine into old wineskins, or else the wineskins break, the wine is spilled, and the wineskins are ruined. But they put new wine into new wineskins, and both are preserved. (Matthew 9:16–17)

Their Eyes Were Opened

And when He had come into the house, the blind men came to Him. And Jesus said to them, "Do you believe that I am able to do this?" They said to Him, "Yes, Lord." Then He touched their eyes, saying, "According to your faith let it be to you." And their eyes were opened. (Matthew 9:28–30)

Power to Heal

He gave them power over unclean spirits, to cast them out, and to heal all kinds of sickness and all kinds of disease.

(Matthew 10:1)

Will Be Saved

But he who endures to the end will be saved.

(Matthew 10:22)

Nothing Covered

For there is nothing covered that will not be revealed, and hidden that will not be known.

(Matthew 10:26)

Confess before My Father

Therefore whoever confesses Me before men, him I will also confess before My Father who is in heaven.

(Matthew 10:32)

Will Find It

He who finds his life will lose it, and he who loses his life for My sake will find it.   (Matthew 10:39)

Find the Higher Life

Whoever finds his [lower] life will lose [the higher life], and whoever loses his [lower] life on My account will find it [the higher life].

(Matthew 10:39 AMP)

Receive Reward

He who receives a prophet in the name of a prophet shall receive a prophet's reward. And he who receives a righteous man in the name of a righteous man shall receive a righteous man's reward. And whoever gives one of these little ones only a cup of cold water in the name of a disciple, assuredly, I say to you, he shall by no means lose his reward. (Matthew 10:41–42)

He Who Is Least Is Greater

Assuredly, I say to you, among those born of women there has not risen one greater than John the Baptist; but he who is least in the kingdom of heaven is greater than he. (Matthew 11:11)

Violent Take It by Force

And from the days of John the Baptist until now the kingdom of heaven suffers violence, and the violent take it by force. (Matthew 11:12)

Burden Is Light

Come to Me, all you who labor and are heavy laden, and I will give you rest. Take My yoke upon you and learn from Me, for I am gentle and lowly in heart, and you will find rest for your souls. For My yoke is easy and My burden is light. (Matthew 11:28–30)

Come to Me, all you who labor and are heavy-laden and overburdened, and I will cause you to rest. [I will ease and relieve and refresh your souls.] Take My yoke upon you and learn of Me, for I am gentle (meek) and humble (lowly) in heart, and you will find rest (relief and ease and refreshment and recreation and blessed quiet) for your souls. For My yoke is wholesome (useful, good—not harsh, hard, sharp, or pressing, but comfortable, gracious, and pleasant, and My burden is light and easy to be borne. (Matthew 11:28–30 AMP)

Lord Even of the Sabbath

For the Son of Man is Lord even of the Sabbath. (Matthew 12:8)

Heart Brings Forth Good Things

For out of the abundance of the heart the mouth speaks. A good man out of the good treasure of his heart brings forth good things, and an evil man out of the evil treasure brings forth evil things. (Matthew 12:34–35)

For out of the fullness (the overflow, the superabundance) of the heart the mouth speaks. The good man from his inner good treasure flings forth good things, and the evil man out of his inner evil storehouse flings forth evil things. But I tell you, on the day of judgment men will have to give account for every idle (inoperative, nonworking) word they speak. (Matthew 12:34–36 AMP)

Will of My Father

For whoever does the will of My Father in heaven is My brother and sister and mother. (Matthew 12:50)

He Will Have Abundance

For whoever has, to him more will be given, and he will have abundance; but whoever does not have, even what he has will be taken away from him. (Matthew 13:12)

Eyes See

But blessed are your eyes for they see, and your ears for they hear. (Matthew 13:16)

Bears Fruit and Produces

When anyone hears the word of the kingdom, and does not understand it, then the wicked one comes and snatches away what was sown in his heart. This is he who received seed by the wayside. But he who received the seed on stony places, this is he who hears the word and immediately receives it with joy; yet he has no root in himself, but endures only for a while. For when tribulation or persecution arises because of the word, immediately he stumbles. Now he who received seed among the thorns is he who hears the word, and the cares of this world and the deceitfulness of riches choke the word, and he becomes unfruitful. But he who received seed on the good ground is he who hears the word and understands it, who indeed bears fruit and produces; some a hundredfold, some sixty, some thirty.

(Matthew 13:19–23)

Righteous Will Shine Forth

Then the righteous will shine forth as the sun in the kingdom of their Father. He who has ears to hear, let him hear!

(Matthew 13:43)

Lame Walking

Then great multitudes came to Him, having with them the lame, blind, mute, maimed, and many others; and they laid them down at Jesus' feet, and He healed them. So the multitude marveled when they saw the mute speaking, the maimed made whole, the lame walking, and the blind seeing; and they glorified the God of Israel.

(Matthew 15:30–31)

Keys of the Kingdom

And I will give you the keys of the kingdom of heaven, and whatever you bind on earth will be bound in heaven, and whatever you loose on earth will be loosed in heaven.

(Matthew 16:19)

Shall Find Life Everlasting

If anyone desires to come after Me, let him deny himself, and take up his cross, and follow Me. For whoever desires to save his life will lose it, but whoever loses his life for My sake will find it.

(Matthew 16:24–25)

Then Jesus said to His disciples, If anyone desires to be My disciple, let him deny himself [disregard, lose sight of, and forget himself and his own interests] and take up his cross and follow Me [cleave steadfastly to Me, conform wholly to My example in living and, if need be, in dying, also]. For whoever is bent on saving his [temporal] life [his comfort and security here] shall lose it [eternal life]; and whoever loses his life [his comfort and security here] for My sake shall find it [life everlasting].

(Matthew 16:24–25 AMP)

I Am Well Pleased

While he was still speaking, behold, a bright cloud overshadowed them; and suddenly a voice came out of the cloud, saying, "This is My beloved Son, in whom I am well pleased. Hear Him!" (Matthew 17:5)

Nothing Will Be Impossible for You

For assuredly, I say to you, if you have faith as a mustard seed, you will say to this mountain, "Move from here to there," and it will move; and nothing will be impossible for you.   (Matthew 17:20)

Receives Me

Therefore whoever humbles himself as this little child is the greatest in the kingdom of heaven. Whoever receives one little child like this in My name receives Me.   (Matthew 18:4–5)

Come to Save

For the Son of Man has come to save that which was lost. (Matthew 18:11)

If Two of You Agree

Assuredly, I say to you, whatever you bind on earth will be bound in heaven, and whatever you loose on earth will be loosed in heaven. Again I say to you that if two of you agree on earth concerning anything that they ask, it will be done for them by My Father in heaven. (Matthew 18:18–19)

I Am There in the Midst of Them

For where two or three are gathered together in My name, I am there in the midst of them. (Matthew 18:20)

The Kingdom of Heaven

But Jesus said, "Let the little children come to Me, and do not forbid them; for of such is the kingdom of heaven." (Matthew 19:14)

All Things Are Possible

But Jesus looked at them and said to them, "With men this is impossible, but with God all things are possible." (Matthew 19:26)

Receive a Hundred Times

And anyone who gives up his home, brothers, sisters, father, mother, wife, children, or property, to follow me, shall receive a hundred times as much in return, and shall have eternal life.

(Matthew 19:29 TLB)

The First Will Be Last

So the last will be first, and the first last.

(Matthew 20:16)

Comes in the Name of the Lord

Hosanna to the Son of David! "Blessed is He who comes in the name of the LORD!"   (Matthew 21:9)

Believing, You Will Receive

If you have faith and do not doubt, you will not only do what was done to the fig tree, but also if you say to this mountain, "Be removed and be cast into the sea," it will be done. And whatever things you ask in prayer, believing, you will receive.

(Matthew 21:21–22)

The End Will Come

But he who endures to the end shall be saved. And this gospel of the kingdom will be preached in all the world as a witness to all the nations, and then the end will come.

(Matthew 24:13–14)

Coming on the Clouds of Heaven

Then the sign of the Son of Man will appear in heaven, and then all the tribes of the earth will mourn, and they will see the Son of Man coming on the clouds of heaven with power and great glory. And He will send His angels with a great sound of a trumpet, and they will gather together His elect from the four winds, from one end of heaven to the other.   (Matthew 24:30–31)

My Words

Heaven and earth will pass away, but My words will by no means pass away.   (Matthew 24:35)

Enter into the Joy of Your Lord

Well done, good and faithful servant; you were faithful over a few things, I will make you ruler over many things. Enter into the joy of your lord.   (Matthew 25:21)

You Did It to Me

Assuredly, I say to you, inasmuch as you did it to one of the least of these My brethren, you did it to Me.   (Matthew 25:40)

He Is Risen

And behold, there was a great earthquake; for an angel of the Lord descended from heaven, and came and rolled back the stone from the door, and sat on it. His countenance was like lightning, and his clothing as white as snow. And the guards shook for fear of him, and became like dead men. But the angel answered and said to the women, "Do not be afraid, for I know that you seek Jesus who was crucified. He is not here; for He is risen, as He said. Come, see the place where the Lord lay."
                                                    (Matthew 28:2–6)

I Am with You Always

"All authority has been given to Me in heaven and on earth. Go therefore and make disciples of all the nations, baptizing them in the name of the Father and of the Son and of the Holy Spirit, teaching them to observe all things that I have commanded you; and lo, I am with you always, even to the end of the age." Amen. (Matthew 28:18–20)

Promises from Micah

Who Walks Uprightly

Do not My words do good to him who walks uprightly? (Micah 2:7)

We May Walk in His Paths

But in the latter days it shall come to pass that the mountain of the house of the Lord shall be established as the highest of the mountains; and it shall be exalted above the hills, and peoples shall flow to it. And many nations shall come and say, Come, let us go up to the mountain of the Lord, to the house of the God of Jacob, that He may teach us His ways, and we may walk in His paths. (Micah 4:1–2 AMP)

Righteousness of the Lord

I redeemed you from the house of bondage;…that you may know the righteousness of the LORD. (Micah 6:4–5)

My God Will Hear Me

Therefore I will look to the Lord; I will wait for the God of my salvation; my God will hear me.

(Micah 7:7)

I Will Arise

When I fall, I will arise.

(Micah 7:8)

Delights in Mercy

He does not retain His anger forever, because He delights in mercy.

(Micah 7:18)

Promises from Nahum

The Clouds Are the Dust of His Feet

The Lord is slow to anger and great in power and will by no means clear the guilty. The Lord has His way in the whirlwind and in the storm, and the clouds are the dust of His feet. (Nahum 1:3 AMP)

Will Not Rise Up a Second Time

The Lord is good, a stronghold in the day of trouble; and He knows those who trust in Him. But with an overflowing flood He will make an utter end of its place, and darkness will pursue His enemies. What do you conspire against the Lord? He will make an utter end of it. Affliction will not rise up a second time.

(Nahum 1:7–9)

Those Who Take Refuge

The Lord is good, a Strength and Stronghold in the day of trouble; He knows (recognizes, has knowledge of, and understands) those who take refuge and trust in Him. (Nahum 1:7 AMP)

Promises from Nehemiah

Will Prosper Us

The God of heaven Himself will prosper us. (Nehemiah 2:20)

Our God

Our God will fight for us. (Nehemiah 4:20)

Joy Is Your Strength

For the joy of the LORD is your strength. (Nehemiah 8:10)

You Alone Are the Lord

Stand up and bless the LORD your God forever and ever! Blessed be Your glorious name, which is exalted above all blessing and praise! You alone are the LORD; You have made heaven, the heaven of heavens, with all their host, the earth and all things on it, the seas and all that is in them, and You preserve them all. The host of heaven worships You. (Nehemiah 9:5–6)

Promises from Numbers

Give You Peace

The LORD bless you and keep you; the LORD make His face shine upon you, and be gracious to you; the LORD lift up His countenance upon you, and give you peace. (Numbers 6:24–26)

Forgiving

The LORD is longsuffering and abundant in mercy, forgiving iniquity and transgression (Numbers 14:18)

Filled with the Glory of the Lord

Truly, as I live, all the earth shall be filled with the glory of the LORD. (Numbers 14:21)

I Am

I am the LORD your God. (Numbers 15:41)

Not a Man, That He Should Lie

God is not a man, that He should lie, nor a son of man, that He should repent. Has He said, and will He not do? Or has He spoken, and will He not make it good? (Numbers 23:19)

Promises from Obadiah

It Shall Be Done to You

For the day of the LORD upon all the nations is near; as you have done, it shall be done to you.
(Obadiah 15)

The Kingdom

Then saviors shall come to Mount Zion to judge the mountains of Esau, and the kingdom shall be the Lord's.
(Obadiah 21)

Promises from 1 Peter

The Priceless Gift of Eternal Life

All honor to God, the God and Father of our Lord Jesus Christ; for it is his boundless mercy that has given us the privilege of being born again, so that we are now members of God's own family. Now we live in the hope of eternal life because Christ rose again from the dead. And God has reserved for his children the priceless gift of eternal life; it is kept in heaven for you, pure and undefiled, beyond the reach of change and decay. And God, in his mighty power, will make sure that you get there safely to receive it, because you are trusting him. It will be yours in that coming last day for all to see.
(1 Peter 1:3–5 TLB)

The Salvation of Your Souls

Without having seen Him, you love Him; though you do not [even] now see Him, you believe in Him and exult and thrill with inexpressible and glorious (triumphant, heavenly) joy. [At the same time] you receive the result (outcome, consummation) of your faith, the salvation of your souls.

(1 Peter 1:8–9 AMP)

Invited You to Be His Child

But be holy now in everything you do, just as the Lord is holy, who invited you to be his child.

(1 Peter 1:15 TLB)

He Paid for You

God paid a ransom to save you from the impossible road to heaven which your fathers tried to take, and the ransom he paid was not mere gold or silver, as you very well know. But he paid for you with the precious lifeblood of Christ, the sinless, spotless Lamb of God.

(1 Peter 1:18-19 TLB)

Gospel Endures Forever

You have been regenerated (born again) not from a mortal origin (seed, sperm) but from one that is immortal by the ever living and lasting Word of God. For all flesh (mankind) is like grass, and all its glory (honor) like [the] flower of grass. The grass withers and the flower drops off, but the Word of the Lord (divine instruction, the Gospel) endures forever. And this Word is the good news which was preached to you.

(1 Peter 1:23–25 AMP)

Never Disappoint

As the Scriptures express it, "See, I am sending Christ to be the carefully chosen, precious Cornerstone of my church, and I will never disappoint those who trust in him." (1 Peter 2:6 TLB)

Out of Darkness into Marvelous Light

But you are a chosen generation, a royal priesthood, a holy nation, His own special people, that you may proclaim the praises of Him who called you out of darkness into His marvelous light. (1 Peter 2:9)

By Whose Stripes You Were Healed

[Jesus] Himself bore our sins in His own body on the tree, that we, having died to sins, might live for righteousness; by whose stripes you were healed. (1 Peter 2:24)

Eyes of the Lord Are upon the Righteous

For the eyes of the Lord are upon the righteous (those who are upright and in right standing with God), and His ears are attentive to their prayer. (1 Peter 3:12 AMP)

Made Alive by the Spirit

For Christ also suffered once for sins, the just for the unjust, that He might bring us to God, being put to death in the flesh but made alive by the Spirit. (1 Peter 3:18)

Powers of Heaven Obeying Him

And now Christ is in heaven, sitting in the place of honor next to God the Father, with all the angels and powers of heaven bowing before him and obeying him. (1 Peter 3:22 TLB)

As God Lives

That is why the Good News was preached even to those who were dead—killed by the flood—so that although their bodies were punished with death, they could still live in their spirits as God lives. (1 Peter 4:6 TLB)

The Ability That God Supplies

If anyone speaks, let him speak as the oracles of God. If anyone ministers, let him do it as with the ability which God supplies, that in all things God may be glorified through Jesus Christ, to whom belong the glory and the dominion forever and ever. Amen. (1 Peter 4:11)

The Spirit of Glory Is Resting upon You

If you are censured and suffer abuse [because you bear] the name of Christ, blessed [are you—happy, fortunate, to be envied, with life-joy, and satisfaction in God's favor and salvation, regardless of your outward condition], because the Spirit of glory, the Spirit of God, is resting upon you. (1 Peter 4:14 AMP)

Crown of Glory

And when the Chief Shepherd appears, you will receive the crown of glory that does not fade away. (1 Peter 5:4)

Grace to the Humble

God resists the proud, but gives grace to the humble.   (1 Peter 5:5)

Everything That Concerns You

Let him have all your worries and cares, for he is always thinking about you and watching everything that concerns you.   (1 Peter 5:7 TLB)

Stronger than Ever

Our God, who is full of kindness through Christ, will give you his eternal glory. He personally will come and pick you up, and set you firmly in place, and make you stronger than ever.
                                                                        (1 Peter 5:10 TLB)

Promises from 2 Peter

Partakers of the Divine Nature

Grace and peace be multiplied to you in the knowledge of God and of Jesus our Lord, as His divine power has given to us all things that pertain to life and godliness, through the knowledge of Him who called us by glory and virtue, by which have been given to us exceedingly great and precious promises, that through these you may be partakers of the divine nature, having escaped the corruption that is in the world through lust.   (2 Peter 1:2–4)

Be neither Barren nor Unfruitful

For if these things are yours and abound, you will be neither barren nor unfruitful in the knowledge of our Lord Jesus Christ. (2 Peter 1:8)

You Will Never Fall

Therefore, my brothers, be all the more eager to make your calling and election sure. For if you do these things, you will never fall, and you will receive a rich welcome into the eternal kingdom of our Lord and Savior Jesus Christ. (2 Peter 1:10–11 NIV)

Deliver the Godly

The Lord knows how to deliver the godly out of temptations. (2 Peter 2:9)

Come to Repentance

With the Lord one day is as a thousand years, and a thousand years as one day. The Lord is not slack concerning His promise, as some count slackness, but is longsuffering toward us, not willing that any should perish but that all should come to repentance. (2 Peter 3:8–9)

A New Heaven and a New Earth

And so since everything around us is going to melt away, what holy, godly lives we should be living! You should look forward to that day and hurry it along—the day when God will set the heavens on fire, and the heavenly bodies will melt and disappear in flames. But we are looking forward to God's promise of new heavens and a new earth afterwards, where there will be only goodness. (2 Peter 3:11–13 TLB)

Promises from Philemon

Grace to You and Peace

Grace to you and peace from God our Father and the Lord Jesus Christ.   (Philemon 3 NIV)

Refreshed the Hearts of Saints

I hear about your faith in the Lord Jesus and your love for all the saints. I pray that you may be active in sharing your faith, so that you will have a full understanding of every good thing we have in Christ. Your love has given me great joy and encouragement, because you, brother, have refreshed the hearts of the saints.   (Philemon 5–7 NIV)

Promises from Philippians

His Fullest Blessings

I pray that God our Father and the Lord Jesus Christ will give each of you his fullest blessings, and his peace in your hearts and your lives.   (Philippians 1:2 TLB)

Finally Finished

And I am sure that God who began the good work within you will keep right on helping you grow in his grace until his task within you is finally finished on that day when Jesus Christ returns.

(Philippians 1:6 TLB)

Overflow with Love for Others

My prayer for you is that you will overflow more and more with love for others, and at the same time keep on growing in spiritual knowledge and insight, for I want you always to see clearly the difference between right and wrong, and to be inwardly clean, no one being able to criticize you from now until our Lord returns.

(Philippians 1:9–10 TLB)

To Live Is Christ

For to me, to live is Christ, and to die is gain.

(Philippians 1:21)

Mind in You

Let this mind be in you which was also in Christ Jesus.

(Philippians 2:5)

Jesus Christ Is Lord

Therefore God also has highly exalted Him and given Him the name which is above every name, that at the name of Jesus every knee should bow, of those in heaven, and of those on earth, and of those under the earth, and that every tongue should confess that Jesus Christ is Lord, to the glory of God the Father.

(Philippians 2:9–11)

Helping You

For God is at work within you, helping you want to obey him, and then helping you do what he wants. (Philippians 2:13 TLB)

Counting on Christ Alone

But all these things that I once thought very worthwhile—now I've thrown them all away so that I can put my trust and hope in Christ alone. Yes, everything else is worthless when compared with the priceless gain of knowing Christ Jesus my Lord. I have put aside all else, counting it worth less than nothing, in order that I can have Christ, and become one with him, no longer counting on being saved by being good enough or by obeying God's laws, but by trusting Christ to save me; for God's way of making us right with himself depends on faith—counting on Christ alone. (Philippians 3:7–9 TLB)

Receive the Prize

So, whatever it takes, I will be one who lives in the fresh newness of life of those who are alive from the dead. No, dear brothers, I am still not all I should be but I am bringing all my energies to bear on this one thing: Forgetting the past and looking forward to what lies ahead, I strain to reach the end of the race and receive the prize for which God is calling us up to heaven because of what Christ Jesus did for us. (Philippians 3:11, 13–14 TLB)

Homeland Is in Heaven

But our homeland is in heaven, where our Savior the Lord Jesus Christ is; and we are looking forward to his return from there. When he comes back he will take these dying bodies of ours and change them into glorious bodies like his own, using the same mighty power that he will use to conquer all else everywhere. (Philippians 3:20–21 TLB)

Experience God's Peace

Always be full of joy in the Lord; I say it again, rejoice! Let everyone see that you are unselfish and considerate in all you do. Remember that the Lord is coming soon. Don't worry about anything; instead, pray about everything; tell God your needs and don't forget to thank him for his answers. If you do this you will experience God's peace, which is far more wonderful than the human mind can understand. His peace will keep your thoughts and your hearts quiet and at rest as you trust in Christ Jesus. (Philippians 4:4–7 TLB)

The God of Peace Will Be with You

And now, brothers, as I close this letter let me say this one more thing: Fix your thoughts on what is true and good and right. Think about things that are pure and lovely, and dwell on the fine, good things in others. Think about all you can praise God for and be glad about. Keep putting into practice all you learned from me and saw me doing, and the God of peace will be with you. (Philippians 4:8–9 TLB)

I Can Do All Things

I can do all things through Christ who strengthens me. (Philippians 4:13)

I can do everything God asks me to with the help of Christ who gives me the strength and power. (Philippians 4:13 TLB)

Supply All

And my God shall supply all your need according to His riches in glory by Christ Jesus. (Philippians 4:19)

Promises from Proverbs

Godly Wisdom

That people may know skillful and godly Wisdom and instruction, discern and comprehend the words of understanding and insight, receive instruction in wise dealing and the discipline of wise thoughtfulness, righteousness, justice, and integrity, that prudence may be given to the simple, and knowledge, discretion, and discernment to the youth—the wise also will hear and increase in learning, and the person of understanding will acquire skill and attain to sound counsel [so that he may be able to steer his course rightly]. (Proverbs 1:2–5 AMP)

The Beginning of Knowledge

The fear of the LORD is the beginning of knowledge, but fools despise wisdom and instruction. (Proverbs 1:7)

Pour Out My Spirit

Surely, I will pour out my spirit on you; I will make my words known to you. (Proverbs 1:23)

Without Fear of Evil

Whoever listens to me will dwell safely, and will be secure, without fear of evil. (Proverbs 1:33)

Lord Grants Wisdom

Every young man who listens to me and obeys my instructions will be given wisdom and good sense. Yes, if you want better insight and discernment, and are searching for them as you would for lost money or hidden treasure, then wisdom will be given you, and knowledge of God himself; you will soon learn the importance of reverence for the Lord and of trusting him. For the Lord grants wisdom! His every word is a treasure of knowledge and understanding. He grants good sense to the godly—his saints. He is their shield, protecting them and guarding their pathway. He shows how to distinguish right from wrong, how to find the right decision every time. For wisdom and truth will enter the very center of your being, filling your life with joy.   (Proverbs 2:1–10 TLB)

Forget Not

My son, forget not my law or teaching, but let your heart keep my commandments; for length of days and years of a life [worth living] and tranquility [inward and outward and continuing through old age till death], these shall they add to you.   (Proverbs 3:1–2 AMP)

Crown Your Efforts with Success

My son, never forget the things I've taught you. If you want a long and satisfying life, closely follow my instructions. Never forget to be truthful and kind. Hold these virtues tightly. Write them deep within your heart. If you want favor with both God and man, and a reputation for good judgment and common sense, then trust the Lord completely; don't ever trust yourself. In everything you do, put God first, and he will direct you and crown your efforts with success.   (Proverbs 3:1–6 TLB)

Health to Your Flesh

Trust in the LORD with all your heart, and lean not on your own understanding; in all your ways acknowledge Him, and He shall direct your paths. Do not be wise in your own eyes; fear the LORD and depart from evil. It will be health to your flesh, and strength to your bones. Honor the LORD with your possessions, and with the firstfruits of all your increase; so your barns will be filled with plenty, and your vats will overflow with new wine.   (Proverbs 3:5–10)

Happy Are All Who Retain Her

Happy is the man who finds wisdom, and the man who gains understanding; for her proceeds are better than the profits of silver, and her gain than fine gold. She is more precious than rubies, and all the things you may desire cannot compare with her. Length of days is in her right hand, in her left hand riches and honor. Her ways are ways of pleasantness, and all her paths are peace. She is a tree of life to those who take hold of her, and happy are all who retain her.   (Proverbs 3:13–18)

He Protects You

Have two goals: wisdom—that is, knowing and doing right—and common sense. Don't let them slip away, for they fill you with living energy and bring you honor and respect. They keep you safe from defeat and disaster and from stumbling off the trail. With them on guard you can sleep without fear; you need not be afraid of disaster or the plots of wicked men, for the Lord is with you; he protects you.   (Proverbs 3:21-24 TLB)

Will Keep Your Foot

Do not be afraid of sudden terror, nor of trouble from the wicked when it comes; for the LORD will be your confidence, and will keep your foot from being caught.   (Proverbs 3:25–26)

Blessings

The curse of the Lord is in and on the house of the wicked, but He declares blessed (joyful and favored with blessings) the home of the just and consistently righteous.   (Proverbs 3:33 AMP)

Gives Grace to the Humble

He...gives grace to the humble. The wise shall inherit glory, but shame shall be the legacy of fools.   (Proverbs 3:34–35)

Retain My Words

Let your heart retain my words; keep my commands, and live. Get wisdom! Get understanding! Do not forget, nor turn away from the words of my mouth.   (Proverbs 4:4–5)

A Crown of Glory

Wisdom is the principal thing; therefore get wisdom. And in all your getting, get understanding. Exalt her, and she will promote you; she will bring you honor, when you embrace her. She will place on your head an ornament of grace; a crown of glory she will deliver to you.   (Proverbs 4:7–9)

The Wisest Life There Is

My son, listen to me and do as I say, and you will have a long, good life. I would have you learn this great fact: that a life of doing right is the wisest life there is.   (Proverbs 4:10–11 TLB)

You Will Not Stumble

Hear, my son, and receive my sayings, and the years of your life will be many. I have taught you in the way of wisdom; I have led you in right paths. When you walk, your steps will not be hindered, and when you run, you will not stumble. (Proverbs 4:10–12)

She Is Your Life

Take firm hold of instruction, do not let go; keep her, for she is your life. (Proverbs 4:13)

Shines Ever Brighter

But the path of the just is like the shining sun, that shines ever brighter unto the perfect day. (Proverbs 4:18)

They Are Life

My son, give attention to my words; incline your ear to my sayings. Do not let them depart from your eyes; keep them in the midst of your heart; for they are life to those who find them, and health to all their flesh. (Proverbs 4:20–22)

Lips May Keep Knowledge

My son, pay attention to my wisdom; lend your ear to my understanding, that you may preserve discretion, and that your lips may keep knowledge. (Proverbs 5:1–2)

The Words of Your Mouth

You are snared by the words of your own mouth; you are taken by the words of your mouth.

(Proverbs 6:2)

They Will Speak with You

My son, keep your father's command, and do not forsake the law of your mother. Bind them continually upon your heart; tie them around your neck. When you roam, they will lead you; when you sleep, they will keep you; and when you awake, they will speak with you. (Proverbs 6:20–22)

He Must Restore Sevenfold

People do not despise a thief if he steals to satisfy himself when he is starving. Yet when he is found, he must restore sevenfold. (Proverbs 6:30–31)

Obey Me and Live

Follow my advice, my son; always keep it in mind and stick to it. Obey me and live! Guard my words as your most precious possession. Write them down, and also keep them deep within your heart. (Proverbs 7:1–3 TLB)

Treasure Them

My son, keep my words; lay up with you my commandments [for use when needed] and treasure them. Keep my commandments and live, and keep my law and teaching as the apple (the pupil) of your eye. Bind them upon your fingers; write them on the tablet of your heart. (Proverbs 7:1–3 AMP)

Mouth Will Speak Truth

Listen, for I will speak of excellent things, and from the opening of my lips will come right things; for my mouth will speak truth. (Proverbs 8:6–7)

All the Words of My Mouth Are with Righteousness

All the words of my mouth are with righteousness; nothing crooked or perverse is in them. They are all plain to him who understands, and right to those who find knowledge. Receive my instruction, and not silver, and knowledge rather than choice gold; for wisdom is better than rubies, and all the things one may desire cannot be compared with her. (Proverbs 8:8–11)

Inherit True Riches

I love those who love me, and those who seek me early and diligently shall find me. Riches and honor are with me, enduring wealth and righteousness (uprightness in every area and relation, and right standing with God). My fruit is better than gold, yes, than refined gold, and my increase than choice silver. I [Wisdom] walk in the way of righteousness (moral and spiritual rectitude in every area and relation), in the midst of the paths of justice, that I may cause those who love me to inherit [true] riches and that I may fill their treasuries. (Proverbs 8:17–21 AMP)

Fill Their Treasuries

Riches and honor are with me, enduring riches and righteousness. My fruit is better than gold, yes, than fine gold, and my revenue than choice silver. I traverse the way of righteousness, in the midst of the paths of justice, that I may cause those who love me to inherit wealth, that I may fill their treasuries. (Proverbs 8:18–21)

Hear and Be Wise

The LORD possessed me at the beginning of His way, before His works of old. I have been established from everlasting, from the beginning, before there was ever an earth. When there were no depths I was brought forth, when there were no fountains abounding with water. Before the mountains were settled, before the hills, I was brought forth; while as yet He had not made the earth or the fields, or the primeval dust of the world. When He prepared the heavens, I was there, when He drew a circle on the face of the deep, when He established the clouds above, when He strengthened the fountains of the deep, when He assigned to the sea its limit, so that the waters would not transgress His command, when He marked out the foundations of the earth, then I was beside Him as a master craftsman; and I was daily His delight, rejoicing always before Him, rejoicing in His inhabited world, and my delight was with the sons of men. Now therefore, listen to me, my children, for blessed are those who keep my ways. Hear instruction and be wise, and do not disdain it. (Proverbs 8:22–33)

Favor from the Lord

Blessed is the man who listens to me, watching daily at my gates, waiting at the posts of my doors. For whoever finds me finds life, and obtains favor from the LORD. (Proverbs 8:34–35)

The Way of Understanding

Forsake foolishness and live, and go in the way of understanding. (Proverbs 9:6)

Days Multiplied

The fear of the LORD is the beginning of wisdom, and the knowledge of the Holy One is understanding. For by me your days will be multiplied, and years of life will be added to you. (Proverbs 9:10–11)

Promises from Proverbs

Good Man

The Lord will not let a good man starve to death, nor will he let the wicked man's riches continue forever. (Proverbs 10:3 TLB)

Memory of the Righteous Is Blessed

Blessings are on the head of the righteous, but violence covers the mouth of the wicked. The memory of the righteous is blessed, but the name of the wicked will rot. (Proverbs 10:6–7)

Walks Securely

He who walks with integrity walks securely. (Proverbs 10:9)

Well of Life

The mouth of the righteous is a well of life, but violence covers the mouth of the wicked. (Proverbs 10:11)

Wisdom Is Found

Wisdom is found on the lips of him who has understanding. (Proverbs 10:13)

A Way of Life

He who heeds instruction and correction is [not only himself] in the way of life, [but also] is a way of life for others. And he who neglects or refuses reproof [not only himself] goes astray [but also] causes to err and is a path toward ruin for others. (Proverbs 10:17 AMP)

Blessing of the Lord

The blessing of the LORD makes one rich, and He adds no sorrow with it. (Proverbs 10:22)

Greatest Wealth

The Lord's blessing is our greatest wealth. All our work adds nothing to it! (Proverbs 10:22 TLB)

Fear, Hope, Way

The fear of the LORD prolongs days, but the years of the wicked will be shortened. The hope of the righteous will be gladness, but the expectation of the wicked will perish. The way of the LORD is strength for the upright, but destruction will come to the workers of iniquity. The righteous will never be removed, but the wicked will not inhabit the earth. The mouth of the righteous brings forth wisdom, but the perverse tongue will be cut out. The lips of the righteous know what is acceptable, but the mouth of the wicked what is perverse. (Proverbs 10:27–32)

Delivered from Trouble

The righteous is delivered from trouble. (Proverbs 11:8)

Multitude of Counselors

Where there is no counsel, the people fall; but in the multitude of counselors there is safety. (Proverbs 11:14)

A Sure Reward

He who sows righteousness will have a sure reward.   (Proverbs 11:18)

His Delight

The blameless in their ways are His delight.   (Proverbs 11:20)

Righteous Will Be Delivered

The posterity of the righteous will be delivered.   (Proverbs 11:21)

Become Richer

It is possible to give away and become richer! It is also possible to hold on too tightly and lose everything. Yes, the liberal man shall be rich! By watering others, he waters himself.

(Proverbs 11:24 TLB)

Finds Favor

He who earnestly seeks good finds favor.   (Proverbs 11:27)

Tree of Life

The fruit of the [uncompromisingly] righteous is a tree of life, and he who is wise captures human lives [for God, as a fisher of men—he gathers and receives them for eternity].   (Proverbs 11:30 AMP)

The fruit of the righteous is a tree of life, and he who wins souls is wise.   (Proverbs 11:30)

Favor

A good man obtains favor from the LORD, but a man of wicked intentions He will condemn.

(Proverbs 12:2)

Will Stand

The wicked are overthrown and are no more, but the house of the righteous will stand.

(Proverbs 12:7)

A Man Will Be Satisfied

A man will be satisfied with good by the fruit of his mouth, and the recompense of a man's hands will be rendered to him.

(Proverbs 12:14)

Counselors of Peace Have Joy

He who speaks truth declares righteousness, but a false witness, deceit. There is one who speaks like the piercings of a sword, but the tongue of the wise promotes health. The truthful lip shall be established forever, but a lying tongue is but for a moment. Deceit is in the heart of those who devise evil, but counselors of peace have joy.

(Proverbs 12:17–20)

Precious Possession

Diligence is man's precious possession.

(Proverbs 12:27)

Preserves Life

He who guards his mouth preserves his life, but he who opens wide his lips shall have destruction.

(Proverbs 13:3)

Shall Be Made Rich

The soul of the diligent shall be made rich.

(Proverbs 13:4)

Whose Way Is Blameless

Righteousness guards him whose way is blameless.

(Proverbs 13:6)

Light Grows Brighter

The light of the [uncompromisingly] righteous [is within him—it grows brighter and] rejoices, but the lamp of the wicked [furnishes only a derived, temporary light and] shall be put out shortly.

(Proverbs 13:9 AMP)

A Good Man

A good man leaves an inheritance to his children's children, but the wealth of the sinner is stored up for the righteous.

(Proverbs 13:22)

Upright Will Flourish

The house of the wicked will be overthrown, but the tent of the upright will flourish.

(Proverbs 14:11)

Godly Man's Life

The backslider gets bored with himself; the godly man's life is exciting. (Proverbs 14:14 TLB)

Holy Thoughts

The backslider in heart [from God and fearing God] shall be filled with [the fruit of] his own ways, and a good man shall be satisfied with [the fruit of] his ways, [with the holy thoughts and actions which his heart prompts and in which he delights]. (Proverbs 14:14 AMP)

Life to the Body

A sound heart is life to the body, but envy is rottenness to the bones. (Proverbs 14:30)

Turns Away Wrath

A soft answer turns away wrath, but a harsh word stirs up anger. (Proverbs 15:1)

Eyes of the Lord

The eyes of the Lord are in every place, keeping watch on the evil and the good. (Proverbs 15:3)

A Tree of Life

A wholesome tongue is a tree of life, but perverseness in it breaks the spirit. (Proverbs 15:4)

Much Treasure

In the house of the righteous there is much treasure, but in the revenue of the wicked is trouble.

(Proverbs 15:6)

His Delight

The prayer of the upright is His delight.

(Proverbs 15:8)

Merry Heart Has a Continual Feast

A merry heart makes a cheerful countenance, but by sorrow of the heart the spirit is broken. The heart of him who has understanding seeks knowledge, but the mouth of fools feeds on foolishness. All the days of the afflicted are evil, but he who is of a merry heart has a continual feast. (Proverbs 15:13–15)

They Are Established

Without counsel, plans go awry, but in the multitude of counselors they are established.

(Proverbs 15:22)

Word Spoken

A man has joy by the answer of his mouth, and a word spoken in due season, how good it is!

(Proverbs 15:23)

Winds Upward

The way of life winds upward for the wise, that he may turn away from hell below. (Proverbs 15:24)

Makes the Bones Healthy

He hears the prayer of the righteous. The light of the eyes rejoices the heart, and a good report makes the bones healthy. (Proverbs 15:29–30)

The Instruction of Wisdom

The fear of the LORD is the instruction of wisdom, and before honor is humility. (Proverbs 15:33)

Your Plans Be Established and Succeed

Roll your works upon the Lord [commit and trust them wholly to Him; He will cause your thoughts to become agreeable to His will, and] so shall your plans be established and succeed. (Proverbs 16:3 AMP)

Departs from Evil

By the fear of the LORD one departs from evil. (Proverbs 16:6)

Enemies at Peace

When a man's ways please the Lord, He makes even his enemies to be at peace with him. (Proverbs 16:7 AMP)

Lord Directs His Steps

A man's heart plans his way, but the LORD directs his steps. (Proverbs 16:9)

Speaks What Is Right

Righteous lips are the delight of kings, and they love him who speaks what is right. (Proverbs 16:13)

To Get Wisdom

How much better it is to get wisdom than gold! And to get understanding is to be chosen rather than silver. (Proverbs 16:16)

Happy, Blessed, and Fortunate

He who deals wisely and heeds [God's] word and counsel shall find good, and whoever leans on, trusts in, and is confident in the Lord—happy, blessed, and fortunate is he. (Proverbs 16:20 AMP)

Health to the Bones

Pleasant words are like a honeycomb, sweetness to the soul and health to the bones. (Proverbs 16:24)

A Crown of Glory

The silver-haired head is a crown of glory, if it is found in the way of righteousness. (Proverbs 16:31)

Grandchildren

An old man's grandchildren are his crowning glory. A child's glory is his father. (Proverbs 17:6 TLB)

A Friend Loves

A friend loves at all times. (Proverbs 17:17)

Merry Heart

A merry heart does good, like medicine, but a broken spirit dries the bones. (Proverbs 17:22)

The Lord Is a Strong Tower

The name of the LORD is a strong tower; the righteous run to it and are safe. (Proverbs 18:10)

In Sickness

The spirit of a man will sustain him in sickness, but who can bear a broken spirit? (Proverbs 18:14)

Man's Gift

A man's gift makes room for him and brings him before great men. (Proverbs 18:16 AMP)

Power of the Tongue

Death and life are in the power of the tongue, and those who love it will eat its fruit. (Proverbs 18:21)

Obtains Favor

He who finds a wife finds a good thing, and obtains favor from the LORD. (Proverbs 18:22)

Will Find Good

He who gets wisdom loves his own soul; he who keeps understanding will find good. (Proverbs 19:8)

His Favor

His favor is like dew on the grass. (Proverbs 19:12)

Wife Is from the Lord

Houses and riches are an inheritance from fathers, but a prudent wife is from the LORD. (Proverbs 19:14)

You May Be Wise

Listen to counsel and receive instruction, that you may be wise in your latter days. (Proverbs 19:20)

The Lord's Counsel

There are many plans in a man's heart, nevertheless the Lord's counsel; that will stand. (Proverbs 19:21)

Rest Satisfied

The reverent, worshipful fear of the Lord leads to life, and he who has it rests satisfied; he cannot be visited with [actual] evil. (Proverbs 19:23 AMP)

His Children Are Blessed after Him

The righteous man walks in his integrity; his children are blessed after him. (Proverbs 20:7)

He Will Save You

Do not say, "I will recompense evil"; wait for the LORD, and He will save you. (Proverbs 20:22)

The Lamp of the Lord

The spirit of a man is the lamp of the LORD, searching all the inner depths of his heart.

(Proverbs 20:27)

Glory

The glory of young men is their strength, and the beauty of old men is their gray head [suggesting wisdom and experience]. (Proverbs 20:29 AMP)

Lead Surely to Plenty

The plans of the diligent lead surely to plenty, but those of everyone who is hasty, surely to poverty.

(Proverbs 21:5)

Will Find Life

He who earnestly seeks after and craves righteousness, mercy, and loving-kindness will find life in addition to righteousness (uprightness and right standing with God) and also honor.

(Proverbs 21:21 AMP)

Keeps His Soul from Troubles

Whoever guards his mouth and tongue keeps his soul from troubles.   (Proverbs 21:23)

A Good Name

A good name is to be chosen rather than great riches, loving favor rather than silver and gold.

(Proverbs 22:1)

Riches and Honor and Life

By humility and the fear of the LORD are riches and honor and life.   (Proverbs 22:4)

He Will Not Depart from It

Train up a child in the way he should go, and when he is old he will not depart from it.

(Proverbs 22:6)

Trust May Be in the Lord

Incline your ear and hear the words of the wise, and apply your heart to my knowledge; for it is a pleasant thing if you keep them within you; let them all be fixed upon your lips, so that your trust may be in the LORD.   (Proverbs 22:17–19)

Godly Wisdom

Through skillful and godly Wisdom is a house (a life, a home, a family) built, and by understanding it is established [on a sound and good foundation].   (Proverbs 24:3 AMP)

And Rise Again

For a righteous man may fall seven times and rise again. (Proverbs 24:16)

A Right Answer

He who gives a right answer kisses the lips. (Proverbs 24:26)

Apples of God

A word fitly spoken is like apples of gold in settings of silver. Like an earring of gold and an ornament of fine gold is a wise rebuker to an obedient ear. Like the cold of snow in time of harvest is a faithful messenger to those who send him, for he refreshes the soul of his masters. (Proverbs 25:11–13)

Lord Will Reward You

If your enemy is hungry, give him bread to eat; and if he is thirsty, give him water to drink; for so you will heap coals of fire on his head, and the Lord will reward you. (Proverbs 25:21–22)

Will Be Honored

Whoever keeps the fig tree will eat its fruit; so he who waits on his master will be honored. (Proverbs 27:18)

Always Reverent

Happy is the man who is always reverent. (Proverbs 28:14)

Abound with Blessings

A faithful man will abound with blessings.   (Proverbs 28:20)

Who Gives to the Poor

He who gives to the poor will not lack.   (Proverbs 28:27)

Delight to Your Soul

Correct your son, and he will give you rest; yes, he will give delight to your soul.   (Proverbs 29:17)

Blessed, Happy, Fortunate Is He

Where there is no vision [no redemptive revelation of God], the people perish; but he who keeps the law [of God, which includes that of man]—blessed (happy, fortunate, and enviable) is he.

(Proverbs 29:18 AMP)

Be Safe

The fear of man brings a snare, but whoever trusts in the LORD shall be safe.   (Proverbs 29:25)

He Is a Shield

Every word of God is pure; He is a shield to those who put their trust in Him.   (Proverbs 30:5)

She Does Him Good

Who can find a virtuous wife? For her worth is far above rubies. The heart of her husband safely trusts her; so he will have no lack of gain. She does him good and not evil all the days of her life.

(Proverbs 31:10–12)

Children Call Her Blessed

Strength and honor are her clothing; she shall rejoice in time to come. She opens her mouth with wisdom, and on her tongue is the law of kindness. She watches over the ways of her household, and does not eat the bread of idleness. Her children rise up and call her blessed. (Proverbs 31:25–28)

A Woman Who Fears the Lord

A woman who fears the LORD, she shall be praised. (Proverbs 31:30)

Promises from the Psalms

Shall Prosper

Blessed is the man who walks not in the counsel of the ungodly, nor stands in the path of sinners, nor sits in the seat of the scornful; but his delight is in the law of the LORD, and in His law he meditates day and night. He shall be like a tree planted by the rivers of water, that brings forth its fruit in its season, whose leaf also shall not wither; and whatever he does shall prosper. (Psalm 1:1–3)

Ask of Me

Ask of Me, and I will give You the nations for Your inheritance, and the ends of the earth for Your possession.

(Psalm 2:8)

Trust in Him

Blessed are all those who put their trust in Him.

(Psalm 2:12)

He Heard Me from His Holy Hill

But You, O LORD, are a shield for me, my glory and the One who lifts up my head. I cried to the LORD with my voice, and He heard me from His holy hill. Selah

(Psalm 3:3–4)

Salvation

Salvation belongs to the LORD. Your blessing is upon Your people. Selah

(Psalm 3:8)

Perfect

O God, you have declared me perfect in your eyes; you have always cared for me in my distress; now hear me as I call again. Have mercy on me. Hear my prayer.

(Psalm 4:1 TLB)

Lord Will Hear

But know that the LORD has set apart for Himself him who is godly; the LORD will hear when I call to Him.

(Psalm 4:3)

Dwell in Safety

I will both lie down in peace, and sleep; for You alone, O LORD, make me dwell in safety. (Psalm 4:8)

Protected by Mercy and Love

But as for me, I will come into your Temple protected by your mercy and your love; I will worship you with deepest awe. (Psalm 5:7 TLB)

Favor

But let all those rejoice who put their trust in You; let them ever shout for joy, because You defend them; let those also who love Your name be joyful in You. For You, O LORD, will bless the righteous; with favor You will surround him as with a shield. (Psalm 5:11–12)

Lord Will Receive

Depart from me, all you workers of iniquity; for the LORD has heard the voice of my weeping. The LORD has heard my supplication; the LORD will receive my prayer. (Psalm 6:8–9)

Integrity

The LORD shall judge the peoples; judge me, O LORD, according to my righteousness, and according to my integrity within me. (Psalm 7:8)

Defend Me

God is my shield; he will defend me. He saves those whose hearts and lives are true and right. (Psalm 7:10 TLB)

Overflows the Heavens

O Lord our God, the majesty and glory of your name fills all the earth and overflows the heavens.

(Psalm 8:1 TLB)

Fills the Earth

O Jehovah, our Lord, the majesty and glory of your name fills the earth.

(Psalm 8:9 TLB)

Forever

But the LORD shall endure forever.

(Psalm 9:7)

Refuge

All who are oppressed may come to him. He is a refuge for them in their times of trouble.

(Psalm 9:9 TLB)

Never Forsaken

All those who know your mercy, Lord, will count on you for help. For you have never yet forsaken those who trust in you.

(Psalm 9:10 TLB)

King Forever

The Lord is King forever and forever. Those who follow other gods shall be swept from his land.

(Psalm 10:16 TLB)

Rules from Heaven

But the Lord is still in his holy temple; he still rules from heaven. He closely watches everything that happens here on earth.

(Psalm 11:4 TLB)

God Is Good

For God is good, and he loves goodness; the godly shall see his face.

(Psalm 11:7 TLB)

Pure Words

The words of the LORD are pure words, like silver tried in a furnace of earth, purified seven times.

(Psalm 12:6)

Bountifully

But I have trusted in Your mercy; my heart shall rejoice in Your salvation. I will sing to the LORD, because He has dealt bountifully with me.

(Psalm 13:5–6)

Love

God is with those who love him.

(Psalm 14:5 TLB)

Abide in His Taberncacle

LORD, who may abide in Your tabernacle? Who may dwell in Your holy hill? He who walks uprightly, and works righteousness, and speaks the truth in his heart.

(Psalm 15:1–2)

True Nobility

I want the company of the godly men and women in the land; they are the true nobility.

(Psalm 16:3 TLB)

My Inheritance

The Lord himself is my inheritance, my prize. He is my food and drink, my highest joy! He guards all that is mine. He sees that I am given pleasant brooks and meadows as my share! What a wonderful inheritance! I will bless the Lord who counsels me; he gives me wisdom in the night. He tells me what to do. I am always thinking of the Lord; and because he is so near, I never need to stumble or to fall. Heart, body, and soul are filled with joy.

(Psalm 16:5–9 TLB)

Fullness of Joy

You will show me the path of life; in Your presence is fullness of joy.

(Psalm 16:11)

Protect

Protect me as you would the pupil of your eye; hide me in the shadow of your wings as you hover over me.

(Psalm 17:8 TLB)

Fully Satisfied

But as for me, my contentment is not in wealth but in seeing you and knowing all is well between us. And when I awake in heaven, I will be fully satisfied, for I will see you face to face. (Psalm 17:15 TLB)

I Am Saved from All My Enemies

The Lord is my fort where I can enter and be safe; no one can follow me in and slay me. He is a rugged mountain where I hide; he is my Savior, a rock where none can reach me, and a tower of safety. He is my shield. He is like the strong horn of a mighty fighting bull. All I need to do is cry to him—oh, praise the Lord—and I am saved from all my enemies!

(Psalm 18:2–3 TLB)

He Rescued Me

He reached down from heaven and took me and drew me out of my great trials. He rescued me from deep waters. He delivered me from my strong enemy, from those who hated me—I who was helpless in their hands. On the day when I was weakest, they attacked. But the Lord held me steady. He led me to a place of safety, for he delights in me. The Lord rewarded me for doing right and being pure. For I have followed his commands and have not sinned by turning back from following him.

(Psalm 18:16–21 TLB)

All His Promises Prove True

Lord, how merciful you are to those who are merciful. And you do not punish those who run from evil. You give blessings to the pure but pain to those who leave your paths. You deliver the humble but condemn the proud and haughty ones. You have turned on my light! The Lord my God has made my darkness turn to light. Now in your strength I can scale any wall, attack any troop. What a God he is! How perfect in every way! All his promises prove true. He is a shield for everyone who hides behind him.

(Psalm 18:25–30 TLB)

Promises from the Psalms

Sets Me on My High Places

It is God who arms me with strength, and makes my way perfect. He makes my feet like the feet of deer, and sets me on my high places. (Psalm 18:32–33)

I Need Never Slip

You have made wide steps beneath my feet so that I need never slip. (Psalm 18:36 TLB)

Strong Armor

For you have armed me with strong armor for the battle. My enemies quail before me and fall defeated at my feet. (Psalm 18:39 TLB)

He Delivers Me

The LORD lives! Blessed be my Rock! Let the God of my salvation be exalted. It is God who avenges me, and subdues the peoples under me; He delivers me from my enemies. You also lift me up above those who rise against me. (Psalm 18:46–48)

Success to Those Who Obey Them

The heavens are telling the glory of God; they are a marvelous display of his craftsmanship. Day and night they keep on telling about God. Without a sound or word, silent in the skies, their message reaches out to all the world. The sun lives in the heavens where God placed it and moves out across the skies as radiant as a bridegroom going to his wedding, or as joyous as an athlete looking forward to a race! The sun crosses the heavens from end to end, and nothing can hide from its heat. God's laws are perfect. They protect us, make us wise, and give us joy and light. God's laws are pure, eternal, just. They are more desirable than gold. They are sweeter than honey dripping from a honeycomb. For they warn us away from harm and give success to those who obey them. (Psalm 19:1–11 TLB)

My Strength

Let the words of my mouth and the meditation of my heart be acceptable in Your sight, O Lord, my strength and my Redeemer. (Psalm 19:14)

We Have Risen

Now I know that the Lord saves His anointed; He will answer him from His holy heaven with the saving strength of His right hand. Some trust in chariots, and some in horses; but we will remember the name of the Lord our God. They have bowed down and fallen; but we have risen and stand upright. (Psalm 20:6–8)

My Shepherd

The LORD is my shepherd; I shall not want. He makes me to lie down in green pastures; He leads me beside the still waters. He restores my soul; He leads me in the paths of righteousness for His name's sake. Yea, though I walk through the valley of the shadow of death, I will fear no evil; for You are with me; Your rod and Your staff, they comfort me. You prepare a table before me in the presence of my enemies; You anoint my head with oil; my cup runs over. Surely goodness and mercy shall follow me all the days of my life; and I will dwell in the house of the LORD forever. (Psalm 23:1–6)

The World Is His

The earth belongs to God! Everything in all the world is his! He is the one who pushed the oceans back to let dry land appear. Who may climb the mountain of the Lord and enter where he lives? Who may stand before the Lord? Only those with pure hands and hearts, who do not practice dishonesty and lying. They will receive God's own goodness as their blessing from him, planted in their lives by God himself, their Savior. (Psalm 24:1–5 TLB)

King of Glory

Lift up your heads, O you gates! And be lifted up, you everlasting doors! And the King of glory shall come in. Who is this King of glory? The LORD strong and mighty, the LORD mighty in battle. Lift up your heads, O you gates! Lift up, you everlasting doors! And the King of glory shall come in. Who is this King of glory? The LORD of hosts, he is the King of glory. Selah (Psalm 24:7–10)

Faith in God

None who have faith in God will ever be disgraced for trusting him. But all who harm the innocent shall be defeated. (Psalm 25:3 TLB)

Dwell in Prosperity

Who is the man that fears the LORD? Him shall He teach in the way He chooses. He himself shall dwell in prosperity, and his descendants shall inherit the earth. The secret of the LORD is with those who fear Him, and He will show them His covenant. (Psalm 25:12–14)

My Light and My Salvation

The LORD is my light and my salvation; whom shall I fear? The LORD is the strength of my life; of whom shall I be afraid? When the wicked came against me to eat up my flesh, my enemies and foes, they stumbled and fell. Though an army may encamp against me, my heart shall not fear; though war should rise against me, in this I will be confident. (Psalm 27:1–3)

My Head Shall Be Lifted Up

For in the time of trouble He shall hide me in His pavilion; in the secret place of His tabernacle He shall hide me; He shall set me high upon a rock. And now my head shall be lifted up above my enemies all around me. (Psalm 27:5–6)

Strengthen Your Heart

Wait on the LORD; be of good courage, and He shall strengthen your heart; wait, I say, on the LORD! (Psalm 27:14)

Full of Majesty

The voice of the LORD is over the waters; the God of glory thunders; the LORD is over many waters. The voice of the LORD is powerful; the voice of the LORD is full of majesty. (Psalm 29:3–4)

Bless with Peace

The LORD will give strength to His people; the LORD will bless His people with peace. (Psalm 29:11)

You Healed Me

O LORD my God, I cried out to You, and You healed me. (Psalm 30:2)

Joy Comes in the Morning

For His anger is but for a moment, His favor is for life; weeping may endure for a night, but joy comes in the morning. (Psalm 30:5)

My Mourning into Dancing

You have turned for me my mourning into dancing; You have put off my sackcloth and clothed me with gladness, to the end that my glory may sing praise to You and not be silent. O LORD my God, I will give thanks to You forever. (Psalm 30:11–12)

Great Is Your Goodness

Oh, how great is your goodness to those who publicly declare that you will rescue them. For you have stored up great blessings for those who trust and reverence you. (Psalm 31:19 TLB)

He Shall Strengthen Your Heart

Be of good courage, and He shall strengthen your heart, all you who hope in the LORD. (Psalm 31:24)

My Hiding Place

You are my hiding place from every storm of life; you even keep me from getting into trouble! You surround me with songs of victory. (Psalm 32:7 TLB)

I Will Guide You

I will instruct you and teach you in the way you should go; I will guide you with My eye. (Psalm 32:8)

Abiding Love

Many sorrows come to the wicked, but abiding love surrounds those who trust in the Lord. (Psalm 32:10 TLB)

Earth Is Full of God's Goodness

Rejoice in the LORD, O you righteous! For praise from the upright is beautiful. Praise the LORD with the harp; make melody to Him with an instrument of ten strings. Sing to Him a new song; play skillfully with a shout of joy. For the word of the LORD is right, and all His work is done in truth. He loves righteousness and justice; the earth is full of the goodness of the LORD. (Psalm 33:1–5)

For Every Generation

His own plan stands forever. His intentions are the same for every generation. (Psalm 33:11 TLB)

His Own Inheritance

Blessed is the nation whose God is the LORD, the people He has chosen as His own inheritance.
(Psalm 33:12)

He Will Keep Them from Death

But the eyes of the Lord are watching over those who fear him, who rely upon his steady love. He will keep them from death even in times of famine! (Psalm 33:18–19 TLB)

Delivered Me from All My Fears

I sought the LORD, and He heard me, and delivered me from all my fears. (Psalm 34:4)

Angel Encamps All Around

The angel of the LORD encamps all around those who fear Him, and delivers them. (Psalm 34:7)

The Man Who Trusts in Him

Oh, taste and see that the LORD is good; blessed is the man who trusts in Him! (Psalm 34:8)

Any Good Thing

The young lions lack and suffer hunger; but those who seek the LORD shall not lack any good thing.
(Psalm 34:10)

Gives Attention

For the eyes of the Lord are intently watching all who live good lives, and he gives attention when they cry to him.

(Psalm 34:15 TLB)

Saves Him out of All His Troubles

Yes, the Lord hears the good man when he calls to him for help, and saves him out of all his troubles.

(Psalm 34:17 TLB)

He Rescues

The Lord is close to those whose hearts are breaking; he rescues those who are humbly sorry for their sins.

(Psalm 34:18 TLB)

The Lord Helps

The good man does not escape all troubles—he has them too. But the Lord helps him in each and every one.

(Psalm 34:19 TLB)

Freely Pardoned

But as for those who serve the Lord, he will redeem them; everyone who takes refuge in him will be freely pardoned.

(Psalm 34:22 TLB)

Promises from the Psalms

Prosperity

Let them shout for joy and be glad, who favor my righteous cause; and let them say continually, "Let the LORD be magnified, who has pleasure in the prosperity of His servant." (Psalm 35:27)

You Are Concerned

Your steadfast love, O Lord, is as great as all the heavens. Your faithfulness reaches beyond the clouds. Your justice is as solid as God's mountains. Your decisions are as full of wisdom as the oceans are with water. You are concerned for men and animals alike. (Psalm 36:5–6 TLB)

Constant Love

How precious is your constant love, O God! All humanity takes refuge in the shadow of your wings. You feed them with blessings from your own table and let them drink from your rivers of delight. For you are the Fountain of life; our light is from your Light. (Psalm 36:7–9 TLB)

The Desires of Your Heart

Trust in the LORD, and do good; dwell in the land, and feed on His faithfulness. Delight yourself also in the LORD, and He shall give you the desires of your heart. (Psalm 37:3–4)

He Will Do It

Commit everything you do to the Lord. Trust in him to help you do it, and he will. (Psalm 37:5 TLB)

Abundance of Peace

But the meek shall inherit the earth, and shall delight themselves in the abundance of peace.
(Psalm 37:11)

Eternal Rewards

Day by day the Lord observes the good deeds done by godly men, and gives them eternal rewards. He cares for them when times are hard; even in famine, they will have enough. (Psalm 37:18–19 TLB)

Inherit the Earth

For those blessed by Him shall inherit the earth, but those cursed by Him shall be cut off.
(Psalm 37:22)

Lord Upholds Him with His Hand

The steps of a good man are ordered by the LORD, and He delights in his way. Though he fall, he shall not be utterly cast down; for the LORD upholds him with His hand.   (Psalm 37:23–24)

His Descendants Are Blessed

I have been young, and now am old; yet I have not seen the righteous forsaken, nor his descendants begging bread. He is ever merciful, and lends; and his descendants are blessed.   (Psalm 37:25–26)

They Are Preserved Forever

For the LORD loves justice, and does not forsake His saints; they are preserved forever, but the descendants of the wicked shall be cut off. (Psalm 37:28)

Inherit and Dwell in It Forever

The righteous shall inherit the land, and dwell in it forever. (Psalm 37:29)

Good Counselor

The godly man is a good counselor because he is just and fair and knows right from wrong. (Psalm 37:30–31 TLB)

He Will Honor You

Don't be impatient for the Lord to act! Keep traveling steadily along his pathway and in due season he will honor you with every blessing, and you will see the wicked destroyed. (Psalm 37:34 TLB)

Wonderful Future

But the good man—what a different story! For the good man—the blameless, the upright, the man of peace—he has a wonderful future ahead of him. For him there is a happy ending. (Psalm 37:37 TLB)

He Helps Them and Delivers Them

The Lord saves the godly! He is their salvation and their refuge when trouble comes. Because they trust in him, he helps them and delivers them from the plots of evil men. (Psalm 37:39 TLB)

New Song

I waited patiently for the Lord; and He inclined to me, and heard my cry. He also brought me up out of a horrible pit, out of the miry clay, and set my feet upon a rock, and established my steps. He has put a new song in my mouth; praise to our God; many will see it and fear, and will trust in the Lord.

(Psalm 40:1–3)

Many Blessings

Many blessings are given to those who trust the Lord, and have no confidence in those who are proud, or who trust in idols. O Lord my God, many and many a time you have done great miracles for us, and we are ever in your thoughts. Who else can do such glorious things? No one else can be compared with you. There isn't time to tell of all your wonderful deeds. (Psalm 40:4–5 TLB)

Thinking about Me Right Now

I am poor and needy, yet the Lord is thinking about me right now! (Psalm 40:17 TLB)

Sustain Him on His Sickbed

Blessed is he who considers the poor; the Lord will deliver him in time of trouble. The Lord will preserve him and keep him alive, and he will be blessed on the earth; you will not deliver him to the will of his enemies. The Lord will strengthen him on his bed of illness; you will sustain him on his sickbed. (Psalm 41:1–3)

You Uphold Me

As for me, You uphold me in my integrity, and set me before Your face forever. (Psalm 41:12)

The Lord Will Command His Lovingkindness

The LORD will command His lovingkindness in the daytime, and in the night His song shall be with me; a prayer to the God of my life. (Psalm 42:8)

We Will Not Fear

God is our refuge and strength, a very present help in trouble. Therefore we will not fear, even though the earth be removed, and though the mountains be carried into the midst of the sea; though its waters roar and be troubled, though the mountains shake with its swelling. Selah (Psalm 46:1–3)

Be Still

Be still, and know that I am God; I will be exalted among the nations, I will be exalted in the earth! (Psalm 46:10)

The Very Best for Those He Loves

Come, everyone, and clap for joy! Shout triumphant praises to the Lord! For the Lord, the God above all gods, is awesome beyond words; he is the great King of all the earth. He subdues the nations before us, and will personally select his choicest blessings for his Jewish people—the very best for those he loves. (Psalm 47:1–4 TLB)

The Residence of the Great King

What a glorious sight! See Mount Zion rising north of the city high above the plains for all to see—Mount Zion, joy of all the earth, the residence of the great King. (Psalm 48:2 TLB)

Even to Death

For this is God, our God forever and ever; He will be our guide even to death.   (Psalm 48:14)

Redeem My Soul

But God will redeem my soul from the power of the grave, for He shall receive me. Selah
(Psalm 49:15)

I Will Deliver You

Call upon Me in the day of trouble; I will deliver you, and you shall glorify Me.   (Psalm 50:15)

I Will Show the Salvation of God

Whoever offers praise glorifies Me; and to him who orders his conduct aright I will show the salvation of God.   (Psalm 50:23)

Whiter than Snow

Purge me with hyssop, and I shall be clean; wash me, and I shall be whiter than snow.   (Psalm 51:7)

He Shall Sustain You

Cast your burden on the LORD, and He shall sustain you; He shall never permit the righteous to be moved.   (Psalm 55:22)

God Is for Me

You number my wanderings; put my tears into Your bottle; are they not in Your book? When I cry out to You, then my enemies will turn back; this I know, because God is for me.   (Psalm 56:8–9)

The very day I call for help, the tide of battle turns. My enemies flee! This one thing I know: God is for me! I am trusting God—oh, praise his promises! I am not afraid of anything mere man can do to me! Yes, praise his promises.   (Psalm 56:9–11 TLB)

You Have Delivered My Soul

In God (I will praise His word), in the LORD (I will praise His word), in God I have put my trust; I will not be afraid. What can man do to me? Vows made to You are binding upon me, O God; I will render praises to You, for You have delivered my soul from death. Have You not delivered my feet from falling, that I may walk before God in the light of the living?   (Psalm 56:10–13)

Love As Vast as the Heavens

Your kindness and love are as vast as the heavens. Your faithfulness is higher than the skies.   (Psalm 57:10 TLB)

Shall Tread Down Our Enemies

Through God we will do valiantly, for it is He who shall tread down our enemies.   (Psalm 60:12)

Strong Tower

For You have been a shelter for me, a strong tower from the enemy. I will abide in Your tabernacle forever; I will trust in the shelter of Your wings. Selah   (Psalm 61:3–4)

Upright Shall Glory

The righteous shall be glad in the LORD, and trust in Him. And all the upright in heart shall glory.   (Psalm 64:10)

Paths Drip with Abundance

You crown the year with Your goodness, and Your paths drip with abundance.   (Psalm 65:11)

Wealth and Great Abundance

You sent troops to ride across our broken bodies. We went through fire and flood. But in the end, you brought us into wealth and great abundance.   (Psalm 66:12 TLB)

Daily Loads Us with Benefits

Blessed be the Lord, who daily loads us with benefits, the God of our salvation! Selah (Psalm 68:19)

Give Strength and Power

O God, You are more awesome than Your holy places. The God of Israel is He who gives strength and power to His people. Blessed be God!   (Psalm 68:35)

All Shall Live in Joy

The humble shall see their God at work for them. No wonder they will be so glad! All who seek for God shall live in joy. (Psalm 69:32 TLB)

My Rock and My Fortress

Be my strong refuge, to which I may resort continually; You have given the commandment to save me, for You are my rock and my fortress. (Psalm 71:3)

You Are Holding My Right Hand

You love me! You are holding my right hand! You will keep on guiding me all my life with your wisdom and counsel; and afterwards receive me into the glories of heaven! (Psalm 73:23–24 TLB)

Your Name Is Near

We give thanks to You, O God, we give thanks! For Your wondrous works declare that Your name is near. (Psalm 75:1)

Gave Ear

I cried out to God with my voice; to God with my voice; and He gave ear to me. (Psalm 77:1)

God of Miracles

You are the God of miracles and wonders! You still demonstrate your awesome power. (Psalm 77:14 TLB)

No Good Thing Will He Withhold

For the LORD God is a sun and shield; the LORD will give grace and glory; no good thing will He withhold from those who walk uprightly. (Psalm 84:11)

You Will Help Me

I will call to you whenever trouble strikes, and you will help me. (Psalm 86:7 TLB)

Full of Compassion

But You, O Lord, are a God full of compassion, and gracious, longsuffering and abundant in mercy and truth. (Psalm 86:15)

Glorious Strength

Strong is your arm! Strong is your hand! Your right hand is lifted high in glorious strength. (Psalm 89:13 TLB)

Two Strong Pillars

Your throne is founded on two strong pillars—the one is Justice and the other Righteousness. Mercy and Truth walk before you as your attendants. Blessed are those who hear the joyful blast of the trumpet, for they shall walk in the light of your presence. (Psalm 89:14 TLB)

I Will Not Break

My covenant I will not break, nor alter the word that has gone out of My lips. (Psalm 89:34)

God without Beginning or End

Before the mountains were created, before the earth was formed, you are God without beginning or end. (Psalm 90:2 TLB)

Confidently Trust

He who dwells in the secret place of the Most High shall remain stable and fixed under the shadow of the Almighty [Whose power no foe can withstand]. I will say of the Lord, He is my Refuge and my Fortress, my God; on Him I lean and rely, and in Him I [confidently] trust! (Psalm 91:1–2 AMP)

Give Angels Charge over You

Because you have made the LORD, who is my refuge, even the Most High, your dwelling place, no evil shall befall you, nor shall any plague come near your dwelling; for He shall give His angels charge over you, to keep you in all your ways. In their hands they shall bear you up, lest you dash your foot against a stone. (Psalm 91:9–12)

I Will Satisfy Him

He shall call upon Me, and I will answer him; I will be with him in trouble; I will deliver him and honor him. With long life I will satisfy him, and show him My salvation. (Psalm 91:15–16)

Satisfy Him with a Full Life

For the Lord says, "Because he loves me, I will rescue him; I will make him great because he trusts in my name. When he calls on me I will answer; I will be with him in trouble, and rescue him and honor him. I will satisfy him with a full life and give him my salvation." (Psalm 91:14–16 TLB)

There Is No Unrighteousness in Him

The righteous shall flourish like a palm tree, he shall grow like a cedar in Lebanon. Those who are planted in the house of the LORD shall flourish in the courts of our God. They shall still bear fruit in old age; they shall be fresh and flourishing, to declare that the LORD is upright; He is my rock, and there is no unrighteousness in Him. (Psalm 92:12–15)

The Lord Reigns

The Lord reigns, He is clothed with majesty; the Lord is robed, He has girded Himself with strength and power; the world also is established, that it cannot be moved. Your throne is established from of old; You are from everlasting. (Psalm 93:1–2 AMP)

Blessed Is the Man

Blessed is the man whom You instruct, O LORD, and teach out of Your law, that You may give him rest from the days of adversity, until the pit is dug for the wicked. (Psalm 94:12–13)

The Lord Is Great

Oh come, let us sing to the LORD! Let us shout joyfully to the Rock of our salvation. Let us come before His presence with thanksgiving; let us shout joyfully to Him with psalms. For the LORD is the great God, and the great King above all gods. (Psalm 95:1–3)

He Is Our God

Oh come, let us worship and bow down; let us kneel before the LORD our Maker. For He is our God, and we are the people of His pasture, and the sheep of His hand. Today, if you will hear His voice. (Psalm 95:6–7)

The Lord Made the Heavens

Oh, sing to the LORD a new song! Sing to the LORD, all the earth. Sing to the LORD, bless His name; proclaim the good news of His salvation from day to day. Declare His glory among the nations, His wonders among all peoples. For the LORD is great and greatly to be praised; He is to be feared above all gods. For all the gods of the peoples are idols, but the LORD made the heavens. Honor and majesty are before Him; strength and beauty are in His sanctuary. (Psalm 96:1–6)

He Is Coming to Judge the Earth

Let the heavens rejoice, and let the earth be glad; let the sea roar, and all its fullness; let the field be joyful, and all that is in it. Then all the trees of the woods will rejoice before the LORD. For He is coming, for He is coming to judge the earth. He shall judge the world with righteousness, and the peoples with His truth. (Psalm 96:11–13)

Your Youth, Renewed, Is like the Eagle's

Bless the LORD, O my soul; and all that is within me, bless His holy name! Bless the LORD, O my soul, and forget not all His benefits: who forgives all your iniquities, who heals all your diseases, who redeems your life from destruction, who crowns you with lovingkindness and tender mercies, who satisfies your mouth with good things, so that your youth is renewed like the eagle's. (Psalm 103:1–5)

He Removed Our Transgressions

For as the heavens are high above the earth, so great is His mercy toward those who fear Him; as far as the east is from the west, so far has He removed our transgressions from us.   (Psalm 103:11–12)

Fills the Hungry Soul

For He satisfies the longing soul, and fills the hungry soul with goodness.   (Psalm 107:9)

Healed

He sent His word and healed them, and delivered them from their destructions.   (Psalm 107:20)

Tread Down Our Enemies

Through God we will do valiantly, for it is He who shall tread down our enemies.   (Psalm 108:13)

His Praise Endures Forever

The fear of the LORD is the beginning of wisdom; a good understanding have all those who do His commandments. His praise endures forever.   (Psalm 111:10)

Wealth and Riches in His House

Praise the LORD! Blessed is the man who fears the LORD, who delights greatly in His commandments. His descendants will be mighty on earth; the generation of the upright will be blessed. Wealth and riches will be in his house, and his righteousness endures forever.   (Psalm 112:1–3)

Precious

Precious in the sight of the LORD is the death of His saints. (Psalm 116:15)

Truth Endures Forever

For His merciful kindness is great toward us, and the truth of the LORD endures forever. Praise the LORD! (Psalm 117:2)

He Will Help Me

He is for me! How can I be afraid? What can mere man do to me? The Lord is on my side, he will help me. Let those who hate me beware. (Psalm 118:6–7 TLB)

I Shall Not Die, but Live

I shall not die, but live, and declare the works of the LORD. (Psalm 118:17)

Laws Are My Light

Your laws are both my light and my counselors. (Psalm 119:24 TLB)

Faithfulness Endures to All Generations

Forever, O LORD, Your word is settled in heaven. Your faithfulness endures to all generations; You established the earth, and it abides. They continue this day according to Your ordinances, for all are Your servants. (Psalm 119:89–91)

Light to My Path

Your word is a lamp to my feet and a light to my path. (Psalm 119:105)

Understanding to the Simple

The entrance of Your words gives light; it gives understanding to the simple. (Psalm 119:130)

Law Is Truth

Your righteousness is an everlasting righteousness, and Your law is truth. (Psalm 119:142)

Always Guards You

He will never let me stumble, slip, or fall. For he is always watching, never sleeping. Jehovah himself is caring for you! He is your defender. He protects you day and night. He keeps you from all evil, and preserves your life. He keeps his eye upon you as you come and go, and always guards you. (Psalm 121:3–8 TLB)

Reap Joy

Those who sow tears shall reap joy. Yes, they go out weeping, carrying seed for sowing, and return singing, carrying their sheaves. (Psalm 126:5–6 TLB).

God's Reward

Blessings on all who reverence and trust the Lord—on all who obey him! Their reward shall be prosperity and happiness. Your wife shall be contented in your home. And look at all those children! There they sit around the dinner table as vigorous and healthy as young olive trees. That is God's reward to those who reverence and trust him. (Psalm 128:1–4 TLB)

His Mercy Endures Forever

Oh, give thanks to the LORD, for He is good! For His mercy endures forever. (Psalm 136:1)

Lord Will Perfect

Though I walk in the midst of trouble, You will revive me; You will stretch out Your hand against the wrath of my enemies, and Your right hand will save me. The LORD will perfect that which concerns me; Your mercy, O LORD, endures forever; do not forsake the works of Your hands. (Psalm 138:7–8)

I Can Never Get Away from My God

I can never be lost to your Spirit! I can never get away from my God! If I go up to heaven, you are there; if I go down to the place of the dead, you are there. If I ride the morning winds to the farthest oceans, even there your hand will guide me, your strength will support me. If I try to hide in the darkness, the night becomes light around me. For even darkness cannot hide from God; to you the night shines as bright as day. Darkness and light are both alike to you. (Psalm 139:7–12 TLB)

He Is My Fortress

Bless the Lord who is my immovable Rock. He gives me strength and skill in battle. He is always kind and loving to me; he is my fortress, my tower of strength and safety, my deliverer. He stands before me as a shield. He subdues my people under me. (Psalm 144:1–2 TLB)

Full of Compassion

The LORD is gracious and full of compassion, slow to anger and great in mercy. The LORD is good to all, and His tender mercies are over all His works. (Psalm 145:8–9)

The Lord Lifts the Fallen

The Lord lifts the fallen and those bent beneath their loads. (Psalm 145:14 TLB)

All Generations

Your kingdom is an everlasting kingdom, and Your dominion endures throughout all generations. (Psalm 145:13)

The Lord Takes Pleasure in His People

Let them praise His name with the dance; let them sing praises to Him with the timbrel and harp. For the LORD takes pleasure in His people; He will beautify the humble with salvation. (Psalm 149:3–4)

Promises from Revelation

Blessed Is He Who Reads and Keeps

Blessed is he who reads and those who hear the words of this prophecy, and keep those things which are written in it; for the time is near.

(Revelation 1:3)

Every Eye Will See

Grace to you and peace from Him who is and who was and who is to come, and from the seven Spirits who are before His throne, and from Jesus Christ, the faithful witness, the firstborn from the dead, and the ruler over the kings of the earth. To Him who loved us and washed us from our sins in His own blood, and has made us kings and priests to His God and Father, to Him be glory and dominion forever and ever. Amen. Behold, He is coming with clouds, and every eye will see Him.

(Revelation 1:4–7)

The Beginning and the End

"I am the Alpha and the Omega, the Beginning and the End," says the Lord, "who is and who was and who is to come, the Almighty."

(Revelation 1:8)

His Countenance Was like the Shining Sun

I saw...One like the Son of Man, clothed with a garment down to the feet and girded about the chest with a golden band. His head and hair were white like wool, as white as snow, and His eyes like a flame of fire; His feet were like fine brass, as if refined in a furnace, and His voice as the sound of many waters; He had in His right hand seven stars, out of His mouth went a sharp two-edged sword, and His countenance was like the sun shining in its strength. (Revelation 1:12–16)

I Am Alive Forevermore

Do not be afraid; I am the First and the Last. I am He who lives, and was dead, and behold, I am alive forevermore. Amen. And I have the keys of Hades and of Death. (Revelation 1:17–18)

The Paradise of God

To him who overcomes I will give to eat from the tree of life, which is in the midst of the Paradise of God. (Revelation 2:7)

Shall Not Be Hurt

He who overcomes shall not be hurt by the second death. (Revelation 2:11)

A New Name

To him who overcomes I will give some of the hidden manna to eat. And I will give him a white stone, and on the stone a new name written which no one knows except him who receives it.

(Revelation 2:17)

Power over the Nations

And he who overcomes, and keeps My works until the end, to him I will give power over the nations. (Revelation 2:26)

I Will Confess His Name

He who overcomes shall be clothed in white garments, and I will not blot out his name from the Book of Life; but I will confess his name before My Father and before His angels.   (Revelation 3:5)

No One Can Shut It

See, I have set before you an open door, and no one can shut it; for you have a little strength, have kept My word, and have not denied My name.   (Revelation 3:8)

I Will Write on Him My New Name

Behold, I am coming quickly! Hold fast what you have, that no one may take your crown. He who overcomes, I will make him a pillar in the temple of My God, and he shall go out no more. And I will write on him the name of My God and the name of the city of My God, the New Jerusalem, which comes down out of heaven from My God. And I will write on him My new name.   (Revelation 3:11–12)

I Will Come In to Him

Behold, I stand at the door and knock. If anyone hears My voice and opens the door, I will come in to him and dine with him, and he with Me.   (Revelation 3:20)

Sit with Me on My Throne

To him who overcomes I will grant to sit with Me on My throne, as I also overcame and sat down with My Father on His throne. (Revelation 3:21)

We Shall Reign on the Earth

You are worthy to take the scroll, and to open its seals; for You were slain, and have redeemed us to God by Your blood out of every tribe and tongue and people and nation, and have made us kings and priests to our God; and we shall reign on the earth. (Revelation 5:9–10)

Worthy

Worthy is the Lamb who was slain to receive power and riches and wisdom, and strength and honor and glory and blessing! (Revelation 5:12)

Forever and Ever

Blessing and honor and glory and power be to Him who sits on the throne, and to the Lamb, forever and ever! (Revelation 5:13)

God Will Wipe Away Every Tear

Therefore they are before the throne of God, and serve Him day and night in His temple. And He who sits on the throne will dwell among them. They shall neither hunger anymore nor thirst anymore; the sun shall not strike them, nor any heat; for the Lamb who is in the midst of the throne will shepherd them and lead them to living fountains of waters. And God will wipe away every tear from their eyes. (Revelation 7:15–17)

His Judgments Are Just and True

Hallelujah! Praise the Lord! Salvation is from our God. Honor and authority belong to him alone; for his judgments are just and true.

(Revelation 19:1–2 TLB)

The Wedding Feast of the Lamb

And out of the throne came a voice that said, "Praise our God, all you his servants, small and great, who fear him." Then I heard again what sounded like the shouting of a huge crowd, or like the waves of a hundred oceans crashing on the shore, or like the mighty rolling of great thunder, "Praise the Lord. For the Lord our God, the Almighty, reigns. Let us be glad and rejoice and honor him; for the time has come for the wedding banquet of the Lamb, and his bride has prepared herself. She is permitted to wear the cleanest and whitest and finest of linens." (Fine linen represents the good deeds done by the people of God.) And the angel dictated this sentence to me: "Blessed are those who are invited to the wedding feast of the Lamb!" And he added, "God himself has stated this."

(Revelation 19:5–9 TLB)

King of Kings and Lord of Lords

Now I saw heaven opened, and behold, a white horse. And He who sat on him was called Faithful and True, and in righteousness He judges and makes war. His eyes were like a flame of fire, and on His head were many crowns. He had a name written that no one knew except Himself. He was clothed with a robe dipped in blood, and His name is called The Word of God. And the armies in heaven, clothed in fine linen, white and clean, followed Him on white horses. Now out of His mouth goes a sharp sword, that with it He should strike the nations. And He Himself will rule them with a rod of iron. He Himself treads the winepress of the fierceness and wrath of Almighty God. And He has on His robe and on His thigh a name written: KING OF KINGS AND LORD OF LORDS. (Revelation 19:11–16)

The Word of God

Then I saw heaven opened and a white horse standing there; and the one sitting on the horse was named "Faithful and True"—the one who justly punishes and makes war. His eyes were like flames, and on his head were many crowns. A name was written on his forehead, and only he knew its meaning. He was clothed with garments dipped in blood, and his title was "The Word of God."

(Revelation 19:11–13 TLB)

Shall Reign with Him

Blessed and holy is he who has part in the first resurrection. Over such the second death has no power, but they shall be priests of God and of Christ, and shall reign with Him a thousand years.

(Revelation 20:6)

Behold, I Make All Things New

"And God will wipe away every tear from their eyes; there shall be no more death, nor sorrow, nor crying. There shall be no more pain, for the former things have passed away." Then He who sat on the throne said, "Behold, I make all things new." And He said to me, "Write, for these words are true and faithful."

(Revelation 21:4–5)

He Shall Be My Son

And He said to me, "It is done! I am the Alpha and the Omega, the Beginning and the End. I will give of the fountain of the water of life freely to him who thirsts. He who overcomes shall inherit all things, and I will be his God and he shall be My son."

(Revelation 21:6–7)

Only Names Written in the Lamb's Book of Life

No temple could be seen in the city, for the Lord God Almighty and the Lamb are worshiped in it everywhere. And the city has no need of sun or moon to light it, for the glory of God and of the Lamb illuminate it. Its light will light the nations of the earth, and the rulers of the world will come and bring their glory to it. Its gates never close; they stay open all day long—and there is no night! And the glory and honor of all the nations shall be brought into it. Nothing evil will be permitted in it—no one immoral or dishonest—but only those whose names are written in the Lamb's Book of Life.
(Revelation 21:22–27 TLB)

I Am Coming Soon

And he pointed out to me a river of pure Water of Life, clear as crystal, flowing from the throne of God and the Lamb, coursing down the center of the main street. On each side of the river grew Trees of Life, bearing twelve crops of fruit, with a fresh crop each month; the leaves were used for medicine to heal the nations. There shall be nothing in the city which is evil; for the throne of God and of the Lamb will be there, and his servants will worship him. And they shall see his face; and his name shall be written on their foreheads. And there will be no night there—no need for lamps or sun—for the Lord God will be their light; and they shall reign forever and ever. Then the angel said to me, "These words are trustworthy and true: 'I am coming soon!' God, who tells his prophets what the future holds, has sent his angel to tell you this will happen soon. Blessed are those who believe it and all else written in the scroll."
(Revelation 22:1–7 TLB)

Drink the Water of Life without Charge

Then he instructed me, "Do not seal up what you have written, for the time of fulfillment is near. And when that time comes, all doing wrong will do it more and more; the vile will become more vile; good men will be better; those who are holy will continue on in greater holiness. See, I am coming soon, and my reward is with me, to repay everyone according to the deeds he has done. I am the A and the Z, the Beginning and the End, the First and Last. Blessed forever are all who are washing their robes, to have the right to enter in through the gates of the city, and to eat the fruit from the Tree of Life. Outside the city are those who have strayed away from God, and the sorcerers and the immoral and murderers and idolaters, and all who love to lie, and do so. I, Jesus, have sent my angel to you to tell the churches all these things. I am both David's Root and his Descendant. I am the bright Morning Star. The Spirit and the bride say, 'Come.' Let each one who hears them say the same, 'Come.' Let the thirsty one come—anyone who wants to; let him come and drink the Water of Life without charge. And I solemnly declare to everyone who reads this book: If anyone adds anything to what is written here, God shall add to him the plagues described in this book. And if anyone subtracts any part of these prophecies, God shall take away his share in the Tree of Life, and in the Holy City just described. He who has said all these things declares: Yes, I am coming soon!"

(Revelation 22:10–20 TLB)

Promises from Romans

You Are God's Very Own

This Good News was promised long ago by God's prophets in the Old Testament. It is the Good News about his Son, Jesus Christ our Lord, who came as a human baby, born into King David's royal family line; and by being raised from the dead he was proved to be the mighty Son of God, with the holy nature of God himself. And now, through Christ, all the kindness of God has been poured out upon us undeserving sinners; and now he is sending us out around the world to tell all people everywhere the great things God has done for them, so that they, too, will believe and obey him. And you, dear friends in Rome, are among those he dearly loves; you, too, are invited by Jesus Christ to be God's very own—yes, his holy people. May all God's mercies and peace be yours from God our Father and from Jesus Christ our Lord. (Romans 1:2–7 TLB)

The Just Shall Live by Faith

For I am not ashamed of the gospel of Christ, for it is the power of God to salvation for everyone who believes, for the Jew first and also for the Greek. For in it the righteousness of God is revealed from faith to faith; as it is written, "The just shall live by faith." (Romans 1:16)

No Partiality with God

Glory, honor, and peace to everyone who works what is good, to the Jew first and also to the Greek. For there is no partiality with God. (Romans 2:10–11)

God Declares Us "Not Guilty"

But now God has shown us a different way to heaven—not by "being good enough" and trying to keep his laws, but by a new way (though not new, really, for the Scriptures told about it long ago). Now God says he will accept and acquit us—declare us "not guilty"—if we trust Jesus Christ to take away our sins. And we all can be saved in this same way, by coming to Christ, no matter who we are or what we have been like. Yes, all have sinned; all fall short of God's glorious ideal; yet now God declares us "not guilty" of offending him if we trust in Jesus Christ, who in his kindness freely takes away our sins.   (Romans 3:21–24 TLB)

A Free Gift

So God's blessings are given to us by faith, as a free gift; we are certain to get them whether or not we follow Jewish customs if we have faith like Abraham's, for Abraham is the father of us all when it comes to these matters of faith.   (Romans 4:16 TLB)

So Shall Your Descendants Be

God, who gives life to the dead and calls those things which do not exist as though they did; who, contrary to hope, in hope believed, so that he became the father of many nations, according to what was spoken, "So shall your descendants be."   (Romans 4:17–18)

Peace with God

Therefore, having been justified by faith, we have peace with God through our Lord Jesus Christ.   (Romans 5:1)

The Love of God Poured Out in Our Hearts

Now hope does not disappoint, because the love of God has been poured out in our hearts by the Holy Spirit who was given to us.

(Romans 5:5)

Christ Died for Us

But God demonstrates His own love toward us, in that while we were still sinners, Christ died for us.

(Romans 5:8)

We Shall Be Saved by His Life

For if when we were enemies we were reconciled to God through the death of His Son, much more, having been reconciled, we shall be saved by His life.

(Romans 5:10)

God's Kindness Rules Instead

Before, sin ruled over all men and brought them to death, but now God's kindness rules instead, giving us right standing with God and resulting in eternal life through Jesus Christ our Lord.

(Romans 5:21 TLB)

Share His New Life

Should we keep on sinning when we don't have to? For sin's power over us was broken when we became Christians and were baptized to become a part of Jesus Christ; through his death the power of your sinful nature was shattered. Your old sin-loving nature was buried with him by baptism when he died, and when God the Father, with glorious power, brought him back to life again, you were given his wonderful new life to enjoy. For you have become a part of him, and so you died with him, so to speak, when he died; and now you share his new life, and shall rise as he did. Your old evil desires were nailed to the cross with him; that part of you that loves to sin was crushed and fatally wounded, so that your sin-loving body is no longer under sin's control, no longer needs to be a slave to sin; for when you are deadened to sin you are freed from all its allure and its power over you. And since your old sin-loving nature "died" with Christ, we know that you will share his new life.   (Romans 6:2–8 TLB)

Free from Sin

Knowing this, that our old man was crucified with Him, that the body of sin might be done away with, that we should no longer be slaves of sin. For he who has died has been freed from sin.
(Romans 6:6–7)

Never Die Again

Christ rose from the dead and will never die again. Death no longer has any power over him.
(Romans 6:9 TLB)

For Sin Shall Not Have Dominion over You

For sin shall not have dominion over you, for you are not under law but under grace.   (Romans 6:14)

Gift of God

But now having been set free from sin, and having become slaves of God, you have your fruit to holiness, and the end, everlasting life. For the wages of sin is death, but the gift of God is eternal life in Christ Jesus our Lord. (Romans 6:22–23)

Now You Need No Longer Worry

When your old nature was still active, sinful desires were at work within you, making you want to do whatever God said not to, and producing sinful deeds, the rotting fruit of death. But now you need no longer worry about the Jewish laws and customs because you "died" while in their captivity, and now you can really serve God; not in the old way, mechanically obeying a set of rules, but in the new way, [with all of your hearts and minds]. (Romans 7:5–6 TLB)

Free from the Law of Sin and Death

There is therefore now no condemnation to those who are in Christ Jesus, who do not walk according to the flesh, but according to the Spirit. For the law of the Spirit of life in Christ Jesus has made me free from the law of sin and death. (Romans 8:1–2)

Your Spirit Will Live

Those who let themselves be controlled by their lower natures live only to please themselves, but those who follow after the Holy Spirit find themselves doing those things that please God. Following after the Holy Spirit leads to life and peace, but following after the old nature leads to death, because the old sinful nature within us is against God. It never did obey God's laws and it never will. That's why those who are still under the control of their old sinful selves, bent on following their old evil desires, can never please God. But you are not like that. You are controlled by your new nature if you have the Spirit of God living in you. (And remember that if anyone doesn't have the Spirit of Christ living in him, he is not a Christian at all.) Yet, even though Christ lives within you, your body will die because of sin; but your spirit will live, for Christ has pardoned it.   (Romans 8:5–10 TLB)

Sons of God

For as many as are led by the Spirit of God, these are sons of God.   (Romans 8:14)

Joint Heirs with Christ

And if children, then heirs—heirs of God and joint heirs with Christ.   (Romans 8:17)

All Things Work Together for Good

And we know that all things work together for good to those who love God, to those who are the called according to His purpose.   (Romans 8:28)

God Is for Us

If God is for us, who can be against us?   (Romans 8:31)

Separate Us from the Love of God

Who shall separate us from the love of Christ? Shall tribulation, or distress, or persecution, or famine, or nakedness, or peril, or sword? As it is written: "For Your sake we are killed all day long; we are accounted as sheep for the slaughter." Yet in all these things we are more than conquerors through Him who loved us. For I am persuaded that neither death nor life, nor angels nor principalities nor powers, nor things present nor things to come, nor height nor depth, nor any other created thing, shall be able to separate us from the love of God which is in Christ Jesus our Lord.   (Romans 8:35–39)

Will Not Be Put to Shame

As it is written: "Behold, I lay in Zion a stumbling stone and rock of offense, and whoever believes on Him will not be put to shame."   (Romans 9:33)

Every One Who Believes

Christ is the end of the law for righteousness to everyone who believes.   (Romans 10:4)

Confession Is Made to Salvation

"The word is near you, in your mouth and in your heart" (that is, the word of faith which we preach): that if you confess with your mouth the Lord Jesus and believe in your heart that God has raised Him from the dead, you will be saved. For with the heart one believes unto righteousness, and with the mouth confession is made unto salvation.   (Romans 10:8–10)

No One Will Ever Be Disappointed

For the Scriptures tell us that no one who believes in Christ will ever be disappointed.   (Romans 10:11 TLB)

Shall Be Saved

For "whoever calls on the name of the LORD shall be saved." (Romans 10:13)

Hearing and Hearing

So then faith comes by hearing, and hearing by the word of God. (Romans 10:17)

Never Go Back on His Promise

For God's gifts and his call can never be withdrawn; he will never go back on his promises. (Romans 11:29 TLB)

Everything Comes from God Alone

For everything comes from God alone. Everything lives by his power, and everything is for his glory. To him be glory evermore. (Romans 11:36 TLB)

His Ways Will Really Satisfy You

Don't copy the behavior and customs of this world, but be a new and different person with a fresh newness in all you do and think. Then you will learn from your own experience how his ways will really satisfy you. (Romans 12:2 TLB)

Measure of Faith

For I say, through the grace given to me, to everyone who is among you, not to think of himself more highly than he ought to think, but to think soberly, as God has dealt to each one a measure of faith. (Romans 12:3)

Promises from Romans

I Will Repay Says the Lord

Beloved, do not avenge yourselves, but rather give place to wrath; for it is written, "Vengeance is Mine, I will repay," says the Lord. (Romans 12:19)

You Will Get Along Well

For the policeman does not frighten people who are doing right; but those doing evil will always fear him. So if you don't want to be afraid, keep the laws and you will get along well. (Romans 13:3 TLB)

Nearer than When We First Believed

And do this, knowing the time, that now it is high time to awake out of sleep; for now our salvation is nearer than when we first believed. (Romans 13:11)

We Are the Lord's

For if we live, we live to the Lord; and if we die, we die to the Lord. Therefore, whether we live or die, we are the Lord's. (Romans 14:8)

Every Tongue Confess to God

For it is written, "As I live," says the Lord, "every knee shall bow to me and every tongue confess to God." (Romans 14:11 TLB)

Acceptable to God

For the kingdom of God is not eating and drinking, but righteousness and peace and joy in the Holy Spirit. For he who serves Christ in these things is acceptable to God and approved by men.

(Romans 14:17–18)

Not from Faith

Whatever is not from faith is sin.

(Romans 14:23)

You May Abound in Hope

Now may the God of hope fill you with all joy and peace in believing, that you may abound in hope by the power of the Holy Spirit.

(Romans 15:13)

Promises from Ruth

The Lord Do So to Me

Entreat me not to leave you, or to turn back from following after you; for wherever you go, I will go; and wherever you lodge, I will lodge; your people shall be my people, and your God, my God. Where you die, I will die, and there will I be buried. The LORD do so to me, and more also.　(Ruth 1:16–17)

The Lord Repay Your Work

The LORD repay your work, and a full reward be given you by the LORD God of Israel, under whose wings you have come for refuge.

(Ruth 2:12)

Promises from 1 Samuel

Rock like Our God

There is none holy like the LORD, for there is none besides You, nor is there any rock like our God.

(1 Samuel 2:2)

Guard the Feet of His Saints

The LORD makes poor and makes rich; He brings low and lifts up. He raises the poor from the dust and lifts the beggar from the ash heap, to set them among princes and make them inherit the throne of glory. For the pillars of the earth are the Lord's, and He has set the world upon them. He will guard the feet of His saints, but the wicked shall be silent in darkness.

(1 Samuel 2:7–9)

Horn of His Anointed

He will give strength to His king, and exalt the horn of His anointed.

(1 Samuel 2:10)

Favor

Favor both with the LORD and men.

(1 Samuel 2:26)

I Will Honor

For those who honor Me I will honor. (1 Samuel 2:30)

God Is with You

Then the Spirit of the LORD will come upon you, and you will prophesy with them and be turned into another man. And let it be, when these signs come to you, that you do as the occasion demands; for God is with you. (1 Samuel 10:6–7)

Saving by Many or by Few

For nothing restrains the LORD from saving by many or by few. (1 Samuel 14:6)

Blessed Are You

Blessed are you of the LORD! (1 Samuel 15:13)

Better than Sacrifice

Behold, to obey is better than sacrifice. (1 Samuel 15:22)

The Lord Looks at the Heart

For the Lord does not see as man sees; for man looks at the outward appearance, but the LORD looks at the heart. (1 Samuel 16:7)

The Battle Is the Lord's

You come to me with a sword, with a spear, and with a javelin. But I come to you in the name of the LORD of hosts, the God of the armies of Israel, whom you have defied. This day the LORD will deliver you into my hand, and I will strike you and take your head from you. And this day I will give the carcasses of the camp of the Philistines to the birds of the air and the wild beasts of the earth, that all the earth may know that there is a God in Israel. Then all this assembly shall know that the LORD does not save with sword and spear; for the battle is the Lord's, and He will give you into our hands.

(1 Samuel 17:45–47)

The Lord Was with Him

And David behaved wisely in all his ways, and the LORD was with him.　　　(1 Samuel 18:14)

Peace to All

Peace be to you, peace to your house, and peace to all that you have!　　　(1 Samuel 25:6)

Promises from 2 Samuel

You Are Blessed

You are blessed of the LORD.　　　(2 Samuel 2:5)

A Breakthrough of Water

The LORD has broken through my enemies before me, like a breakthrough of water. (2 Samuel 5:20)

The Lord Is with You

Then Nathan said to the king, "Go, do all that is in your heart, for the LORD is with you."
(2 Samuel 7:3)

Saved from My Enemies

The LORD is my rock and my fortress and my deliverer; the God of my strength, in whom I will trust; my shield and the horn of my salvation, my stronghold and my refuge; my Savior, You save me from violence. I will call upon the LORD, who is worthy to be praised; so shall I be saved from my enemies.   (2 Samuel 22:2–4)

He Heard My Voice

In my distress I called upon the LORD, and cried to my God; He heard my voice from His temple, and my cry entered His ears.   (2 Samuel 22:7)

He Is a Shield

As for God, His way is perfect; the word of the LORD is proven; He is a shield to all who trust in Him.
(2 Samuel 22:31)

He Makes My Way Perfect

God is my strength and power, and He makes my way perfect. He makes my feet like the feet of deer, and sets me on my high places. (2 Samuel 22:33–34)

Promises from Song of Songs

Your Name Is Ointment

Let him kiss me with the kisses of his mouth; for your love is better than wine. Because of the fragrance of your good ointments, your name is ointment poured forth. (Song of Songs 1:2–3)

The Lily of the Valleys

I am the rose of Sharon, and the lily of the valleys. (Song of Songs 2:1)

His Banner over Me Was Love

He brought me to the banqueting house, and his banner over me was love. (Song of Songs 2:4)

I Am His

My beloved is mine, and I am His. (Song of Songs 2:16)

There Is No Spot in You

You are all fair, my love, and there is no spot in you.   (Song of Songs 4:7)

Love Is As Strong as Death

For love is as strong as death, jealousy as cruel as the grave; its flames are flames of fire, a most vehement flame. Many waters cannot quench love, nor can the floods drown it.   (Song of Songs 8:6–7)

Promises from I Thessalonians

Heart Peace

Grace (spiritual blessing and divine favor) to you and [heart] peace.   (1 Thessalonians 1:1 AMP)

He Has Selected (Chosen) You

[O] brethren beloved by God, we recognize and know that He has selected (chosen) you; for our [preaching of the] glad tidings (the Gospel) came to you not only in word, but also in [its own inherent] power and in the Holy Spirit and with great conviction and absolute certainty [on our part]. You know what kind of men we proved [ourselves] to be among you for your good.

(1 Thessalonians 1:4–5 AMP)

Draws Us to Himself

And [how you] look forward to and await the coming of His Son from heaven, Whom He raised from the dead—Jesus, Who personally rescues and delivers us out of and from the wrath [bringing punishment] which is coming [upon the impenitent] and draws us to Himself [investing us with all the privileges and rewards of the new life in Christ, the Messiah].   (1 Thessalonians 1:10 AMP)

Approved by God

But just as we have been approved by God to be entrusted with the glad tidings (the Gospel), so we speak not to please men but to please God, Who tests our hearts [expecting them to be approved].
(1 Thessalonians 2:4 AMP)

Effectively Works in You

For this reason we also thank God without ceasing, because when you received the word of God which you heard from us, you welcomed it not as the word of men, but as it is in truth, the word of God, which also effectively works in you who believe.   (1 Thessalonians 2:13)

It Changed Your Lives

And we will never stop thanking God for this: that when we preached to you, you didn't think of the words we spoke as being just our own, but you accepted what we said as the very Word of God—which, of course, it was—and it changed your lives when you believed it.   (1 Thessalonians 2:13 TLB)

Increase and Excel and Overflow

And may the Lord make you increase and abound in love to one another and to all, just as we do to you, so that He may establish your hearts blameless in holiness before our God and Father at the coming of our LORD Jesus Christ with all His saints. (1 Thessalonians 3:12–13)

And may the Lord make you to increase and excel and overflow in love for one another and for all people, just as we also do for you, so that He may strengthen and confirm and establish your hearts faultlessly pure and unblamable in holiness in the sight of our God and Father, at the coming of our Lord Jesus Christ (the Messiah) with all His saints (the holy and glorified people of God)! Amen (so be it)! (1 Thessalonians 3:12–13 AMP)

Will of God

For this is the will of God, that you should be consecrated (separated and set apart for pure and holy living): that you should abstain and shrink from all sexual vice, that each one of you should know how to possess (control, manage) his own body in consecration (purity, separated from things profane) and honor, not [to be used] in the passion of lust like the heathen, who are ignorant of the true God and have no knowledge of His will. (1 Thessalonians 4:3–5 AMP)

Those Who Sleep

For if we believe that Jesus died and rose again, even so God will bring with Him those who sleep in Jesus. (1 Thessalonians 4:14)

Promises from I Thessalonians

We Shall Be with the Lord

For the Lord Himself will descend from heaven with a shout, with the voice of an archangel, and with the trumpet of God. And the dead in Christ will rise first. Then we who are alive and remain shall be caught up together with them in the clouds to meet the Lord in the air. And thus we shall always be with the Lord. (1 Thessalonians 4:16–17)

Sons of Light

For you are all sons of light and sons of the day; we do not belong either to the night or to darkness. Accordingly then, let us not sleep, as the rest do, but let us keep wide awake (alert, watchful, cautious, and on our guard) and let us be sober (calm, collected, and circumspect). (1 Thessalonians 5:5–6 AMP)

God's Will

Always be joyful. Always keep on praying. No matter what happens, always be thankful, for this is God's will for you who belong to Christ Jesus. (1 Thessalonians 5:16–18 TLB)

The Holy and Glorified People of God

And may the God of peace Himself sanctify you through and through [separate you from profane things, make you pure and wholly consecrated to God]; and may your spirit and soul and body be preserved sound and complete [and found] blameless at the coming of our Lord Jesus Christ (the Messiah). (1 Thessalonians 5:23 AMP)

Faithful Is He

He who calls you is faithful, who also will do it. (1 Thessalonians 5:24)

Faithful is He Who is calling you [to Himself] and utterly trustworthy, and He will also do it [fulfill His call by hallowing and keeping you]. (1 Thessalonians 5:24 AMP)

Promises from 2 Thessalonians

Your Faith Grows Exceedingly

We are bound to thank God always for you, brethren, as it is fitting, because your faith grows exceedingly, and the love of every one of you all abounds toward each other. (2 Thessalonians 1:3)

Because You Have Believed

And so I would say to you who are suffering, God will give you rest along with us when the Lord Jesus appears suddenly from heaven in flaming fire with his mighty angels, bringing judgment on those who do not wish to know God, and who refuse to accept his plan to save them through our Lord Jesus Christ. They will be punished in everlasting hell, forever separated from the Lord, never to see the glory of his power, when he comes to receive praise and admiration because of all he has done for his people, his saints. And you will be among those praising him, because you have believed what we told you about him. (2 Thessalonians 1:7–10 TLB)

God Chose You for Salvation

But we are bound to give thanks to God always for you, brethren beloved by the Lord, because God from the beginning chose you for salvation through sanctification by the Spirit and belief in the truth, to which He called you by our gospel, for the obtaining of the glory of our Lord Jesus Christ.   (2 Thessalonians 2:13–14)

Help You in Every Good Thing

With all these things in mind, dear brothers, stand firm and keep a strong grip on the truth that we taught you in our letters and during the time we were with you. May our Lord Jesus Christ himself and God our Father, who has loved us and given us everlasting comfort and hope, which we don't deserve, comfort your hearts with all comfort, and help you in every good thing you say and do.

(2 Thessalonians 2:15–17 TLB)

Guard You from Satanic Attacks

But the Lord is faithful; he will make you strong and guard you from satanic attacks of every kind.

(2 Thessalonians 3:3 TLB)

Under All Circumstances and Conditions

Now may the Lord of peace Himself grant you His peace (the peace of His kingdom) at all times and in all ways [under all circumstances and conditions, whatever comes]. The Lord [be] with you all.

(2 Thessalonians 3:16 AMP)

Promises from 1 Timothy

To Save Sinners

This is a faithful saying and worthy of all acceptance, that Christ Jesus came into the world to save sinners. (1 Timothy 1:15)

He Alone Is God

But God had mercy on me so that Christ Jesus could use me as an example to show everyone how patient he is with even the worst sinners, so that others will realize that they, too, can have everlasting life. Glory and honor to God forever and ever. He is the King of the ages, the unseen one who never dies; he alone is God, and full of wisdom. Amen. (1 Timothy 1:16–17 TLB)

He Will Save Their Souls

So God sent pain and suffering to women when their children are born, but he will save their souls if they trust in him, living quiet, good, and loving lives. (1 Timothy 2:15 TLB)

The Answer Lies in Christ

It is quite true that the way to live a godly life is not an easy matter. But the answer lies in Christ, who came to earth as a man, was proved spotless and pure in his Spirit, was served by angels, was preached among the nations, was accepted by men everywhere and was received up again to his glory in heaven. (1 Timothy 3:16 TLB)

By the Word of God and Prayer

For everything God made is good, and we may eat it gladly if we are thankful for it, and if we ask God to bless it, for it is made good by the Word of God and prayer.   (1 Timothy 4:4–5 TLB)

Spiritual Exercise Is More Important

Bodily exercise is all right, but spiritual exercise is much more important and is a tonic for all you do. So exercise yourself spiritually, and practice being a better Christian, because that will help you not only now in this life, but in the next life too. This is the truth and everyone should accept it. We work hard and suffer much in order that people will believe it, for our hope is in the living God who died for all, and particularly for those who have accepted his salvation.   (1 Timothy 4:8–9 TLB)

Deserve Their Pay

Pastors who do their work well should be paid well and should be highly appreciated, especially those who work hard at both preaching and teaching. For the Scriptures say, "Never tie up the mouth of an ox when it is treading out the grain—let him eat as he goes along!" And in another place, "Those who work deserve their pay!"   (1 Timothy 5:17–18 TLB)

You Are Happy and Good

Do you want to be truly rich? You already are if you are happy and good. After all, we didn't bring any money with us when we came into the world, and we can't carry away a single penny when we die.   (1 Timothy 6:6–7 TLB)

Christ Will Be Revealed from Heaven

Oh, Timothy, you are God's man. Run from all these evil things and work instead at what is right and good, learning to trust him and love others, and to be patient and gentle. Fight on for God. Hold tightly to the eternal life which God has given you, and which you have confessed with such a ringing confession before many witnesses. I command you before God who gives life to all, and before Christ Jesus who gave a fearless testimony before Pontius Pilate, that you fulfill all he has told you to do, so that no one can find fault with you from now until our Lord Jesus Christ returns. For in due season Christ will be revealed from heaven by the blessed and only Almighty God, the King of kings and Lord of lords, who alone can never die, who lives in light so terrible that no human being can approach him. No mere man has ever seen him, nor ever will. Unto him be honor and everlasting power and dominion forever and ever. Amen. (1 Timothy 6:11–16 TLB)

Gives Us All We Need

Tell those who are rich not to be proud and not to trust in their money, which will soon be gone, but their pride and trust should be in the living God who always richly gives us all we need for our enjoyment. (1 Timothy 6:17 TLB)

The Only Safe Investment for Eternity

Tell them to use their money to do good. They should be rich in good works and should give happily to those in need, always being ready to share with others whatever God has given them. By doing this they will be storing up real treasure for themselves in heaven—it is the only safe investment for eternity! And they will be living a fruitful Christian life down here as well. (1 Timothy 6:18–19 TLB)

Promises from 2 Timothy

Power, Love, and a Sound Mind

For God has not given us a spirit of fear, but of power and of love and of a sound mind.

(2 Timothy 1:7)

Discipline and Self-Control

For God did not give us a spirit of timidity (of cowardice, of craven and cringing and fawning fear), but [He has given us a spirit] of power and of love and of calm and well-balanced mind and discipline and self-control.

(2 Timothy 1:7 AMP)

Everlasting Life through Trusting Him

It is he who saved us and chose us for his holy work, not because we deserved it but because that was his plan long before the world began—to show his love and kindness to us through Christ. And now he has made all of this plain to us by the coming of our Savior Jesus Christ, who broke the power of death and showed us the way of everlasting life through trusting him.

(2 Timothy 1:9–10 TLB)

He Cannot Deny Himself

The saying is sure and worthy of confidence: If we have died with Him, we shall also live with Him. If we endure, we shall also reign with Him. If we deny and disown and reject Him, He will also deny and disown and reject us. If we are faithless [do not believe and are untrue to Him], He remains true (faithful to His Word and His righteous character), for He cannot deny Himself.

(2 Timothy 2:11–13 AMP)

God's Truth Stands Firm

But God's truth stands firm like a great rock, and nothing can shake it. It is a foundation stone with these words written on it: "The Lord knows those who are really his," and "A person who calls himself a Christian should not be doing things that are wrong." In a wealthy home there are dishes made of gold and silver as well as some made from wood and clay. The expensive dishes are used for guests, and the cheap ones are used in the kitchen or to put garbage in. If you stay away from sin you will be like one of these dishes made of purest gold—the very best in the house—so that Christ himself can use you for his highest purposes. Run from anything that gives you the evil thoughts that young men often have, but stay close to anything that makes you want to do right. Have faith and love, and enjoy the companionship of those who love the Lord and have pure hearts.   (2 Timothy 2:19–22 TLB)

Thoroughly Equipped for Good Work

All Scripture is given by inspiration of God, and is profitable for doctrine, for reproof, for correction, for instruction in righteousness, that the man of God may be complete, thoroughly equipped for every good work.

(2 Timothy 3:16–17)

God-Breathed

Every Scripture is God-breathed (given by His inspiration) and profitable for instruction, for reproof and conviction of sin, for correction of error and discipline in obedience, [and] for training in righteousness (in holy living, in conformity to God's will in thought, purpose and action), so that the man of God may be complete and proficient, well fitted and thoroughly equipped for every good work.

(2 Timothy 3:16–17 AMP)

A Crown Is Waiting for Me

In heaven a crown is waiting for me which the Lord, the righteous Judge, will give me on that great day of his return. And not just to me, but to all those whose lives show that they are eagerly looking forward to his coming back again.

(2 Timothy 4:8 TLB)

Promises from Titus

He Cannot Lie

I have been sent to bring faith to those God has chosen and to teach them to know God's truth—the kind of truth that changes lives—so that they can have eternal life, which God promised them before the world began—and he cannot lie.

(Titus 1:1 TLB)

All Things Are Pure

To the pure, all things are pure.

(Titus 1:15 NIV)

It Teaches Us to Say No

For the grace of God that brings salvation has appeared to all men. It teaches us to say "No" to ungodliness and worldly passions, and to live self-controlled, upright and godly lives in this present age, while we wait for the blessed hope—the glorious appearing of our great God and Savior, Jesus Christ, who gave himself for us to redeem us from all wickedness and to purify for himself a people that are his very own, eager to do what is good. (Titus 2:11–14 NIV)

Heirs of Eternal Life

He saved us, not because of any works of righteousness that we had done, but because of His own pity and mercy, by [the] cleansing [bath] of the new birth (regeneration) and renewing of the Holy Spirit, which He poured out [so] richly upon us through Jesus Christ our Savior. [And He did it in order] that we might be justified by His grace (by His favor, wholly undeserved), [that we might be acknowledged and counted as conformed to the divine will in purpose, thought, and action], and that we might become heirs of eternal life according to [our] hope. (Titus 3:5–7 AMP)

Promises from Zechariah

I Will Return to You

"Return to Me," says the LORD of hosts, "and I will return to you," says the LORD of hosts. (Zechariah 1:3)

By My Spirit

"Not by might nor by power, but by My Spirit," says the LORD of hosts.   (Zechariah 4:6)

Rule on His Throne

Behold, the Man whose name is the BRANCH! From His place He shall branch out, and He shall build the temple of the LORD; yes, He shall build the temple of the LORD. He shall bear the glory, and shall sit and rule on His throne; so He shall be a priest on His throne, and the counsel of peace shall be between them both.   (Zechariah 6:12–13)

God Is with You

Thus says the LORD of hosts: "In those days ten men from every language of the nations shall grasp the sleeve of a Jewish man, saying, 'Let us go with you, for we have heard that God is with you.'"   (Zechariah 8:23)

Showers of Rain

Ask the LORD for rain in the time of the latter rain. The LORD will make flashing clouds; He will give them showers of rain, grass in the field for everyone.   (Zechariah 10:1)

The Lord Is My God

I will bring the one-third through the fire, will refine them as silver is refined, and test them as gold is tested. They will call on My name, and I will answer them. I will say, "This is My people"; and each one will say, "The LORD is my God."   (Zechariah 13:9)

King over All the Earth

And in that day it shall be that living waters shall flow from Jerusalem, half of them toward the eastern sea and half of them toward the western sea; in both summer and winter it shall occur. And the LORD shall be King over all the earth. In that day it shall be; "The LORD is one," and His name one.   (Zechariah 14:8–9)

Promises from Zephaniah

He Has Invited His Guests

Be silent in the presence of the Lord GOD; for the day of the LORD is at hand, for the LORD has prepared a sacrifice; He has invited His guests.   (Zephaniah 1:7)

Wait for Me

Therefore [earnestly] wait for Me, says the Lord, [waiting] for the day when I rise up to the attack [as a witness, accuser, or judge, and a testimony]. For My decision and determination and right it is to gather the nations together, to assemble the kingdoms, to pour upon them My indignation, even all [the heat of] My fierce anger; for [in that day] all the earth shall be consumed with the fire of My zeal and jealousy. For then [changing their impure language] I will give to the people a clear and pure speech from pure lips, that they may all call upon the name of the Lord, to serve Him with one unanimous consent and one united shoulder [bearing the yoke of the Lord].   (Zephaniah 3:8–9 AMP)

God Is in the Midst of You

The Lord your God is in the midst of you, a Mighty One, a Savior [Who saves]! He will rejoice over you with joy; He will rest [in silent satisfaction] and in His love He will be silent and make no mention [of past sins, or even recall them]; He will exult over you with singing.   (Zephaniah 3:17 AMP)

Bring You In

At that time I will bring you in; yes, at that time I will gather you, for I will make you a name and a praise among all the nations of the earth when I reverse your captivity before your eyes, says the Lord.   (Zephaniah 3:20 AMP)

Scriptures to Memorize

You Shall Receive Power

But you shall receive power when the Holy Spirit has come upon you; and you shall be witnesses to Me in Jerusalem, and in all Judea and Samaria, and to the end of the earth.   (Acts 1:8)

Whoever Calls Shall Be Saved

And it shall come to pass in the last days, says God, that I will pour out of My Spirit on all flesh; your sons and your daughters shall prophesy, your young men shall see visions, your old men shall dream dreams. And on My menservants and on My maidservants I will pour out My Spirit in those days; and they shall prophesy. I will show wonders in heaven above and signs in the earth beneath: blood and fire and vapor of smoke. The sun shall be turned into darkness, and the moon into blood, before the coming of the great and awesome day of the LORD. And it shall come to pass that whoever calls on the name of the LORD shall be saved. (Acts 2:17–21)

Times of Refreshing May Come

Repent therefore and be converted, that your sins may be blotted out, so that times of refreshing may come from the presence of the Lord. (Acts 3:19)

By Which We Must Be Saved

Nor is there salvation in any other, for there is no other name under heaven given among men by which we must be saved. (Acts 4:12)

Believe on the Lord Jesus Christ

So they said, "Believe on the Lord Jesus Christ, and you will be saved, you and your household." (Acts 16:31)

Unusual Miracles

Now God worked unusual miracles by the hands of Paul, so that even handkerchiefs or aprons were brought from his body to the sick, and the diseases left them and the evil spirits went out of them.

(Acts 19:11–12)

Not Leave You or Forsake You

Be strong and of good courage, and do it; do not fear nor be dismayed, for the LORD God; my God; will be with you. He will not leave you nor forsake you, until you have finished all the work for the service of the house of the LORD.

(1 Chronicles 28:20)

Mercy Endures Forever

Praise the LORD, for His mercy endures forever.

(2 Chronicles 20:21)

Redemption

In whom we have redemption through His blood, the forgiveness of sins.

(Colossians 1:14)

Nothing Left against You

It was through what his Son did that God cleared a path for everything to come to him—all things in heaven and on earth—for Christ's death on the cross has made peace with God for all by his blood. This includes you who were once so far away from God. You were his enemies and hated him and were separated from him by your evil thoughts and actions, yet now he has brought you back as his friends. He has done this through the death on the cross of his own human body, and now as a result Christ has brought you into the very presence of God, and you are standing there before him with nothing left against you—nothing left that he could even chide you for.　　　(Colossians 1:20–22 TLB)

Christ in You

To them God willed to make known what are the riches of the glory of this mystery among the Gentiles: which is Christ in you, the hope of glory.　　　(Colossians 1:27)

Christ's Mighty Energy

This is my work, and I can do it only because Christ's mighty energy is at work within me.　　　(Colossians 1:29 TLB)

You Have Everything When You Have Christ

For in Christ there is all of God in a human body; so you have everything when you have Christ, and you are filled with God through your union with Christ. He is the highest Ruler, with authority over every other power. When you came to Christ, he set you free from your evil desires, not by a bodily operation of circumcision but by a spiritual operation, the baptism of your souls. For in baptism you see how your old, evil nature died with him and was buried with him; and then you came up out of death with him into a new life because you trusted the Word of the mighty God who raised Christ from the dead.   (Colossians 2:9–12 TLB)

From the Lord You Will Receive the Reward

And whatever you do, do it heartily, as to the Lord and not to men, knowing that from the Lord you will receive the reward of the inheritance; for you serve the Lord Christ.   (Colossians 3:23)

The Things God Has Prepared

But as it is written: "Eye has not seen, nor ear heard, nor have entered into the heart of man the things which God has prepared for those who love Him."   (1 Corinthians 2:9)

In Power

For the kingdom of God is not in word but in power.   (1 Corinthians 4:20)

Love Never Fails

Love never fails.   (1 Corinthians 13:8)

Greatest Is Love

And now abide faith, hope, love, these three; but the greatest of these is love.   (1 Corinthians 13:13)

Things Not Seen Are Eternal

We do not look at the things which are seen, but at the things which are not seen. For the things which are seen are temporary, but the things which are not seen are eternal.   (2 Corinthians 4:18)

Walk by Faith

For we walk by faith, not by sight.   (2 Corinthians 5:7)

All Things Have Become New

Therefore, if anyone is in Christ, he is a new creation; old things have passed away; behold, all things have become new.   (2 Corinthians 5:17)

You Might Become Rich

For you know the grace of our Lord Jesus Christ, that though He was rich, yet for your sakes He became poor, that you through His poverty might become rich.   (1 Corinthians 8:9)

You Have an Abundance

But this I say: He who sows sparingly will also reap sparingly, and he who sows bountifully will also reap bountifully. So let each one give as he purposes in his heart, not grudgingly or of necessity; for God loves a cheerful giver. And God is able to make all grace abound toward you, that you, always having all sufficiency in all things, may have an abundance for every good work.

(2 Corinthians 9:6–8)

But remember this—if you give little, you will get little. A farmer who plants just a few seeds will get only a small crop, but if he plants much, he will reap much. Every one must make up his own mind as to how much he should give. Don't force anyone to give more than he really wants to, for cheerful givers are the ones God prizes. God is able to make it up to you by giving you everything you need and more, so that there will not only be enough for your own needs, but plenty left over to give joyfully to others.

(2 Corinthians 9:6–8 TLB)

Take Away All Sickness

You shall be blessed above all peoples; there shall not be a male or female barren among you or among your livestock. And the LORD will take away from you all sickness, and will afflict you with none of the terrible diseases of Egypt which you have known, but will lay them on all those who hate you.
(Deuteronomy 7:14–15)

Power to Get Wealth

And you shall remember the LORD your God, for it is He who gives you power to get wealth, that He may establish His covenant which He swore to your fathers, as it is this day.   (Deuteronomy 8:18)

Choose Life

I call heaven and earth as witnesses today against you, that I have set before you life and death, blessing and cursing; therefore choose life, that both you and your descendants may live.

(Deuteronomy 30:19)

He Will Not Leave You

Be strong and of good courage, do not fear nor be afraid of them; for the LORD your God, He is the One who goes with you. He will not leave you nor forsake you. (Deuteronomy 31:6)

He Has Put Eternity in Their Hearts

He has made everything beautiful in its time. Also He has put eternity in their hearts.

(Ecclesiastes 3:11)

His Mighty Power

Now glory be to God who by his mighty power at work within us is able to do far more than we would ever dare to ask or even dream of—infinitely beyond our highest prayers, desires, thoughts, or hopes. (Ephesians 3:20 TLB)

Full of Blessing

And this is the promise: that if you honor your father and mother, yours will be a long life, full of blessing. (Ephesians 6:3 TLB)

Scriptures to Memorize

Quench All the Fiery Darts of the Wicked One

Put on the whole armor of God, that you may be able to stand against the wiles of the devil. For we do not wrestle against flesh and blood, but against principalities, against powers, against the rulers of the darkness of this age, against spiritual hosts of wickedness in the heavenly places. Therefore take up the whole armor of God, that you may be able to withstand in the evil day, and having done all, to stand. Stand therefore, having girded your waist with truth, having put on the breastplate of righteousness, and having shod your feet with the preparation of the gospel of peace; above all, taking the shield of faith with which you will be able to quench all the fiery darts of the wicked one. And take the helmet of salvation, and the sword of the Spirit, which is the word of God.   (Ephesians 6:11–17)

I Am the Lord Who Heals You

If you diligently heed the voice of the LORD your God and do what is right in His sight, give ear to His commandments and keep all His statutes, I will put none of the diseases on you which I have brought on the Egyptians. For I am the LORD who heals you.   (Exodus 15:26)

Give You a New Heart

I will give you a new heart and put a new spirit within you; I will take the heart of stone out of your flesh and give you a heart of flesh.   (Ezekiel 36:26)

I Have Been Crucified

I have been crucified with Christ: and I myself no longer live, but Christ lives in me. And the real life I now have within this body is a result of my trusting in the Son of God, who loved me and gave himself for me.   (Galatians 2:20 TLB)

Christ Lives in Me

I have been crucified with Christ; it is no longer I who live, but Christ lives in me; and the life which I now live in the flesh I live by faith in the Son of God, who loved me and gave Himself for me.

(Galatians 2:20)

By Faith

But that no one is justified by the law in the sight of God is evident, for "the just shall live by faith."

(Galatians 3:11)

Redeemed from the Curse

Christ has redeemed us from the curse of the law, having become a curse for us (for it is written, "Cursed is everyone who hangs on a tree"), that the blessing of Abraham might come upon the Gentiles in Christ Jesus, that we might receive the promise of the Spirit through faith.   (Galatians 3:13–14)

They Shall Become One Flesh

And the LORD God said, "It is not good that man should be alone; I will make him a helper comparable to him." Out of the ground the LORD God formed every beast of the field and every bird of the air, and brought them to Adam to see what he would call them. And whatever Adam called each living creature, that was its name. So Adam gave names to all cattle, to the birds of the air, and to every beast of the field. But for Adam there was not found a helper comparable to him. And the LORD God caused a deep sleep to fall on Adam, and he slept; and He took one of his ribs, and closed up the flesh in its place. Then the rib which the LORD God had taken from man He made into a woman, and He brought her to the man. And Adam said: "This is now bone of my bones and flesh of my flesh; she shall be called Woman, because she was taken out of Man." Therefore a man shall leave his father and mother and be joined to his wife, and they shall become one flesh.   (Genesis 2:18–24)

Earth Remains

While the earth remains, seedtime and harvest, cold and heat, winter and summer, and day and night shall not cease.   (Genesis 8:22)

I Am Your Shield

I am your shield, your exceedingly great reward.   (Genesis 15:1)

Be Utterly Astounded

Look among the nations and watch; be utterly astounded! For I will work a work in your days which you would not believe, though it were told you.   (Habakkuk 1:5)

As the Waters Cover the Sea

For the earth will be filled with the knowledge of the glory of the LORD, as the waters cover the sea. (Habakkuk 2:14)

Sharper than Any Two-edged Sword

For the word of God is living and powerful, and sharper than any two-edged sword, piercing even to the division of soul and spirit, and of joints and marrow, and is a discerner of the thoughts and intents of the heart. (Hebrews 4:12)

Substance of Things Hoped For

Now faith is the substance of things hoped for, the evidence of things not seen. (Hebrews 11:1)

I Will Not Fear

For He Himself has said, "I will never leave you nor forsake you." So we may boldly say: "The LORD is my helper; I will not fear. What can man do to me?" (Hebrews 13:5–6)

Forever

Jesus Christ is the same yesterday, today, and forever. (Hebrews 13:8)

They Shall Be As White as Snow

Though your sins are like scarlet, they shall be as white as snow; though they are red like crimson, they shall be as wool. If you are willing and obedient, you shall eat the good of the land. (Isaiah 1:18–19)

Word of Our God Stands

The grass withers, the flower fades, but the word of our God stands forever. (Isaiah 40:8)

Those Who Wait on the Lord

Those who wait on the LORD shall renew their strength; they shall mount up with wings like eagles, they shall run and not be weary, they shall walk and not faint. (Isaiah 40:31)

I Will Uphold You

Fear not, for I am with you; be not dismayed, for I am your God. I will strengthen you, yes, I will help you, I will uphold you with My righteous right hand. (Isaiah 41:10)

I Tell You of Them

Behold, the former things have come to pass, and new things I declare; before they spring forth I tell you of them. (Isaiah 42:9)

I Am the Lord Your God

Fear not, for I have redeemed you; I have called you by your name; you are Mine. When you pass through the waters, I will be with you; and through the rivers, they shall not overflow you. When you walk through the fire, you shall not be burned, nor shall the flame scorch you. For I am the LORD your God, the Holy One of Israel, your Savior. (Isaiah 43:1–3)

I Have Inscribed You

See, I have inscribed you on the palms of My hands.

(Isaiah 49:16)

Your God Reigns

How beautiful upon the mountains are the feet of him who brings good news, who proclaims peace, who brings glad tidings of good things, who proclaims salvation, who says to Zion, "Your God reigns!"

(Isaiah 52:7)

By His Stripes We Are Healed

Surely He has borne our griefs and carried our sorrows; yet we esteemed Him stricken, smitten by God, and afflicted. But He was wounded for our transgressions, He was bruised for our iniquities; the chastisement for our peace was upon Him, and by His stripes we are healed.

(Isaiah 53:4–5)

I Impart to Them

"No weapon formed against you shall prosper, and every tongue which rises against you in judgment you shall condemn. This is the heritage of the servants of the LORD, and their righteousness is from Me," says the LORD.

(Isaiah 54:17)

My Ways Higher than Your Ways

"For My thoughts are not your thoughts, nor are your ways My ways," says the LORD. "For as the heavens are higher than the earth, so are My ways higher than your ways, and My thoughts than your thoughts."

(Isaiah 55:8–9)

Shall Not Return to Me Void

For as the rain comes down, and the snow from heaven, and do not return there, but water the earth, and make it bring forth and bud, that it may give seed to the sower and bread to the eater, so shall My word be that goes forth from My mouth; it shall not return to Me void, but it shall accomplish what I please, and it shall prosper in the thing for which I sent it.   (Isaiah 55:10–11)

Lord Will Lift Up a Standard

When the enemy comes in like a flood, the Spirit of the LORD will lift up a standard against him.
(Isaiah 59:19)

Shall Not Depart from Your Mouth

"As for Me," says the LORD, "this is My covenant with them: My Spirit who is upon you, and My words which I have put in your mouth, shall not depart from your mouth, nor from the mouth of your descendants, nor from the mouth of your descendants' descendants," says the LORD, "from this time and forevermore."   (Isaiah 59:21)

A Royal Diadem

You shall be called by a new name, which the mouth of the LORD will name. You shall also be a crown of glory in the hand of the LORD, and a royal diadem in the hand of your God.   (Isaiah 62:2–3)

Before They Call

It shall come to pass that before they call, I will answer; and while they are still speaking, I will hear.
(Isaiah 65:24)

It Will Be Given to Him

If any of you lacks wisdom, he should ask God, who gives generously to all without finding fault, and it will be given to him.
(James 1:5 NIV)

He Will Come Near to You

Submit yourselves, then, to God. Resist the devil, and he will flee from you. Come near to God and he will come near to you. Wash your hands, you sinners, and purify your hearts, you double-minded.
(James 4:7–8 NIV)

Prayer Is Powerful

Is any one of you in trouble? He should pray. Is anyone happy? Let him sing songs of praise. Is any one of you sick? He should call the elders of the church to pray over him and anoint him with oil in the name of the Lord. And the prayer offered in faith will make the sick person well; the Lord will raise him up. If he has sinned, he will be forgiven. Therefore confess your sins to each other and pray for each other so that you may be healed. The prayer of a righteous man is powerful and effective.
(James 5:13–16 NIV)

Dynamic in Its Working

The earnest (heartfelt, continued) prayer of a righteous man makes tremendous power available [dynamic in its working].
(James 5:16 AMP)

Before You Were Born

Before I formed you in the womb I knew you; before you were born I sanctified you.   (Jeremiah 1:5)

Restore Health

"For I will restore health to you and heal you of your wounds," says the Lord.   (Jeremiah 30:17)

Anything Too Hard for Me?

Behold, I am the LORD, the God of all flesh. Is there anything too hard for Me?   (Jeremiah 32:27)

Whoever Calls Shall Be Saved

And it shall come to pass afterward that I will pour out My Spirit on all flesh; your sons and your daughters shall prophesy, your old men shall dream dreams, your young men shall see visions. And also on My menservants and on My maidservants I will pour out My Spirit in those days. And I will show wonders in the heavens and in the earth: blood and fire and pillars of smoke. The sun shall be turned into darkness, and the moon into blood, before the coming of the great and awesome day of the LORD. And it shall come to pass that whoever calls on the name of the LORD shall be saved. (Joel 2:28–32)

Without Him Nothing Was Made

In the beginning was the Word, and the Word was with God, and the Word was God. He was in the beginning with God. All things were made through Him, and without Him nothing was made that was made.   (John 1:1–3)

Who Believe in His Name

But as many as received Him, to them He gave the right to become children of God, to those who believe in His name.   (John 1:12)

The World Might Be Saved

For God so loved the world that He gave His only begotten Son, that whoever believes in Him should not perish but have everlasting life. For God did not send His Son into the world to condemn the world, but that the world through Him might be saved. (John 3:16–17)

Springing Up into Everlasting Life

Jesus answered and said to her, "Whoever drinks of this water will thirst again, but whoever drinks of the water that I shall give him will never thirst. But the water that I shall give him will become in him a fountain of water springing up into everlasting life." (John 4:13–14)

The Bread of Life

And Jesus said to them, "I am the bread of life. He who comes to Me shall never hunger, and he who believes in Me shall never thirst." (John 6:35)

Rivers of Living Water

If anyone thirsts, let him come to Me and drink. He who believes in Me, as the Scripture has said, out of his heart will flow rivers of living water. (John 7:37–38)

Light of the World

Then Jesus spoke to them again, saying, "I am the light of the world. He who follows Me shall not walk in darkness, but have the light of life." (John 8:12)

Truth Shall Make You Free

Then Jesus said to those Jews who believed Him, "If you abide in My word, you are My disciples indeed. And you shall know the truth, and the truth shall make you free." (John 8:31–32)

Free Indeed

Therefore if the Son makes you free, you shall be free indeed. (John 8:36)

Life More Abundantly

The thief does not come except to steal, and to kill, and to destroy. I have come that they may have life, and that they may have it more abundantly. (John 10:10)

I Am the Way

Jesus said to him, "I am the way, the truth, and the life. No one comes to the Father except through Me." (John 14:6)

Greater Works than These He Will Do

Believe Me that I am in the Father and the Father in Me, or else believe Me for the sake of the works themselves. Most assuredly, I say to you, he who believes in Me, the works that I do he will do also; and greater works than these he will do, because I go to My Father. And whatever you ask in My name, that I will do, that the Father may be glorified in the Son. If you ask anything in My name, I will do it. (John 14:11–14)

Neither Let It Be Afraid

Peace I leave with you, My peace I give to you; not as the world gives do I give to you. Let not your heart be troubled, neither let it be afraid. (John 14:27)

Cleanse Us from All Unrighteousness

If we confess our sins, He is faithful and just to forgive us our sins and to cleanse us from all unrighteousness. (1 John 1:9)

He Is Greater

He who is in you is greater than he who is in the world. (1 John 4:4)

Your Soul Prospers

Beloved, I pray that you may prosper in all things and be in health, just as your soul prospers. (3 John 2)

I Have Given You Every Place

Every place that the sole of your foot will tread upon I have given you, as I said to Moses. (Joshua 1:3)

Nor Forsake You

I will not leave you nor forsake you. (Joshua 1:5)

God Is with You

Have I not commanded you? Be strong and of good courage; do not be afraid, nor be dismayed, for the Lord your God is with you wherever you go. (Joshua 1:9)

There Has Not Failed One Word

There has not failed one word of all His good promise. (1 Kings 8:56)

Surely I Will Heal You

I have heard your prayer, I have seen your tears; surely I will heal you. (2 Kings 20:5)

It Is Holy to the Lord

And all the tithe of the land, whether of the seed of the land or of the fruit of the tree, is the Lord's. It is holy to the Lord. (Leviticus 27:30)

No Word from God Shall Be without Power

For with God nothing is ever impossible and no word from God shall be without power or impossible of fulfillment. (Luke 1:37 AMP)

Every Promise Shall Come True

For every promise from God shall surely come true. (Luke 1:37 TLB)

Baptize with Holy Spirit and Fire

John answered, saying to all, "I indeed baptize you with water; but One mightier than I is coming, whose sandal strap I am not worthy to loose. He will baptize you with the Holy Spirit and fire."

(Luke 3:16)

Every Word of God

But Jesus answered him, saying, "It is written, 'Man shall not live by bread alone, but by every word of God.'"

(Luke 4:4)

Will Be Given Back to You

For if you give, you will get! Your gift will return to you in full and overflowing measure, pressed down, shaken together to make room for more, and running over. Whatever measure you use to give—large or small—will be used to measure what is given back to you. (Luke 6:38 TLB)

Your Names Are Written in Heaven

Behold, I give you the authority to trample on serpents and scorpions, and over all the power of the enemy, and nothing shall by any means hurt you. Nevertheless do not rejoice in this, that the spirits are subject to you, but rather rejoice because your names are written in heaven. (Luke 10:19–20)

The Door Shall Be Opened

So I say to you, Ask and keep on asking and it shall be given you; seek and keep on seeking and you shall find; knock and keep on knocking and the door shall be opened to you. For everyone who asks and keeps on asking receives; and he who seeks and keeps on seeking finds; and to him who knocks and keeps on knocking, the door shall be opened. (Luke 11:9–10 AMP)

No Thief Can Steal Them

Wherever your treasure is, there your heart and thoughts will also be. (Luke 12:34 TLB)

Possible with God

But He said, "The things which are impossible with men are possible with God." (Luke 18:27)

Save That Which Was Lost

For the Son of Man has come to seek and to save that which was lost. (Luke 19:10)

Forever True

And though all heaven and earth shall pass away, yet my words remain forever true. (Luke 21:33 TLB)

I Do Not Change

For I am the LORD, I do not change. (Malachi 3:6)

Try Me Now

"Bring all the tithes into the storehouse, that there may be food in My house, and try Me now in this," says the LORD of hosts, "if I will not open for you the windows of heaven and pour out for you such blessing that there will not be room enough to receive it." (Malachi 3:10)

Fishers of Men

Then Jesus said to them, "Follow Me, and I will make you become fishers of men." (Mark 1:17)

All Things Are Possible

Jesus said to him, "If you can believe, all things are possible to him who believes." (Mark 9:23)

Two Shall Become One Flesh

But from the beginning of the creation, God "made them male and female." "For this reason a man shall leave his father and mother and be joined to his wife, and the two shall become one flesh"; so then they are no longer two, but one flesh. Therefore what God has joined together, let not man separate. (Mark 10:6–9)

Possible with God

But Jesus looked at them and said, "With men it is impossible, but not with God; for with God all things are possible." (Mark 10:27)

You Will Have Them

So Jesus answered and said to them, "Have faith in God. For assuredly, I say to you, whoever says to this mountain, 'Be removed and be cast into the sea,' and does not doubt in his heart, but believes that those things he says will be done, he will have whatever he says. Therefore I say to you, whatever things you ask when you pray, believe that you receive them, and you will have them. And whenever you stand praying, if you have anything against anyone, forgive him, that your Father in heaven may also forgive you your trespasses. But if you do not forgive, neither will your Father in heaven forgive your trespasses."

(Mark 11:22–26)

They Will Recover

And He said to them, "Go into all the world and preach the gospel to every creature. He who believes and is baptized will be saved; but he who does not believe will be condemned. And these signs will follow those who believe: In My name they will cast out demons; they will speak with new tongues; they will take up serpents; and if they drink anything deadly, it will by no means hurt them; they will lay hands on the sick, and they will recover."

(Mark 16:15–18)

Baptize You with the Holy Spirit

I indeed baptize you with water unto repentance, but He who is coming after me is mightier than I, whose sandals I am not worthy to carry. He will baptize you with the Holy Spirit and fire.

(Matthew 3:11)

Every Word

But He answered and said, "It is written, 'Man shall not live by bread alone, but by every word that proceeds from the mouth of God.'"

(Matthew 4:4)

Light of the World

You are the light of the world. A city that is set on a hill cannot be hidden. Nor do they light a lamp and put it under a basket, but on a lampstand, and it gives light to all who are in the house. Let your light so shine before men, that they may see your good works and glorify your Father in heaven. (Matthew 5:14–16)

Father in Heaven Is Perfect

Therefore you shall be perfect, just as your Father in heaven is perfect.　　(Matthew 5:48)

Treasures in Heaven

Do not lay up for yourselves treasures on earth, where moth and rust destroy and where thieves break in and steal; but lay up for yourselves treasures in heaven, where neither moth nor rust destroys and where thieves do not break in and steal. (Matthew 6:19-20)

Ask, Seek, Knock

Ask, and it will be given to you; seek, and you will find; knock, and it will be opened to you. For everyone who asks receives, and he who seeks finds, and to him who knocks it will be opened. (Matthew 7:7–8)

Burden Is Light

Come to Me, all you who labor and are heavy laden, and I will give you rest. Take My yoke upon you and learn from Me, for I am gentle and lowly in heart, and you will find rest for your souls. For My yoke is easy and My burden is light. (Matthew 11:28–30)

Keys of the Kingdom

And I will give you the keys of the kingdom of heaven, and whatever you bind on earth will be bound in heaven, and whatever you loose on earth will be loosed in heaven. (Matthew 16:19)

Shall Find Life Everlasting

If anyone desires to come after Me, let him deny himself, and take up his cross, and follow Me. For whoever desires to save his life will lose it, but whoever loses his life for My sake will find it. (Matthew 16:24–25)

Nothing Will Be Impossible for You

For assuredly, I say to you, if you have faith as a mustard seed, you will say to this mountain, "Move from here to there," and it will move; and nothing will be impossible for you. (Matthew 17:20)

If Two of You Agree

Assuredly, I say to you, whatever you bind on earth will be bound in heaven, and whatever you loose on earth will be loosed in heaven. Again I say to you that if two of you agree on earth concerning anything that they ask, it will be done for them by My Father in heaven. (Matthew 18:18–19)

Receive a Hundred Times

And anyone who gives up his home, brothers, sisters, father, mother, wife, children, or property, to follow me, shall receive a hundred times as much in return, and shall have eternal life. (Matthew 19:29 TLB)

Believing, You Will Receive

If you have faith and do not doubt, you will not only do what was done to the fig tree, but also if you say to this mountain, "Be removed and be cast into the sea," it will be done. And whatever things you ask in prayer, believing, you will receive. (Matthew 21:21–22)

My Words

Heaven and earth will pass away, but My words will by no means pass away. (Matthew 24:35)

I Will Arise

When I fall, I will arise. (Micah 7:8)

Will Not Rise Up a Second Time

The Lord is good, a stronghold in the day of trouble; and He knows those who trust in Him. But with an overflowing flood He will make an utter end of its place, and darkness will pursue His enemies. What do you conspire against the Lord? He will make an utter end of it. Affliction will not rise up a second time. (Nahum 1:7–9)

Joy Is Your Strength

For the joy of the Lord is your strength. (Nehemiah 8:10)

Filled with the Glory of the Lord

Truly, as I live, all the earth shall be filled with the glory of the Lord. (Numbers 14:21)

Out of Darkness into Marvelous Light

But you are a chosen generation, a royal priesthood, a holy nation, His own special people, that you may proclaim the praises of Him who called you out of darkness into His marvelous light; who once were not a people but are now the people of God, who had not obtained mercy but now have obtained mercy. (1 Peter 2:9–10)

By Whose Stripes You Were Healed

Who Himself bore our sins in His own body on the tree, that we, having died to sins, might live for righteousness; by whose stripes you were healed. (1 Peter 2:24)

Mind in You

Let this mind be in you which was also in Christ Jesus. (Philippians 2:5)

Jesus Christ Is Lord

Therefore God also has highly exalted Him and given Him the name which is above every name, that at the name of Jesus every knee should bow, of those in heaven, and of those on earth, and of those under the earth, and that every tongue should confess that Jesus Christ is Lord, to the glory of God the Father. (Philippians 2:9–11)

Helping You

For God is at work within you, helping you want to obey him, and then helping you do what he wants. (Philippians 2:13 TLB)

Receive the Prize

So, whatever it takes, I will be one who lives in the fresh newness of life of those who are alive from the dead. No, dear brothers, I am still not all I should be but I am bringing all my energies to bear on this one thing: Forgetting the past and looking forward to what lies ahead, I strain to reach the end of the race and receive the prize for which God is calling us up to heaven because of what Christ Jesus did for us.
(Philippians 3:13–14 TLB)

Experience God's Peace

Always be full of joy in the Lord; I say it again, rejoice! Let everyone see that you are unselfish and considerate in all you do. Remember that the Lord is coming soon. Don't worry about anything; instead, pray about everything; tell God your needs and don't forget to thank him for his answers. If you do this you will experience God's peace, which is far more wonderful than the human mind can understand. His peace will keep your thoughts and your hearts quiet and at rest as you trust in Christ Jesus.
(Philippians 4:4–7 TLB)

I Can Do

I can do all things through Christ who strengthens me.
(Philippians 4:13)

Supply All

And my God shall supply all your need according to His riches in glory by Christ Jesus.
(Philippians 4:19)

Fear of the Lord

The fear of the LORD is the beginning of knowledge, but fools despise wisdom and instruction.

(Proverbs 1:7)

Health to Your Flesh

Trust in the LORD with all your heart, and lean not on your own understanding; in all your ways acknowledge Him, and He shall direct your paths. Do not be wise in your own eyes; fear the LORD and depart from evil. It will be health to your flesh, and strength to your bones. Honor the LORD with your possessions, and with the firstfruits of all your increase; so your barns will be filled with plenty, and your vats will overflow with new wine.

(Proverbs 3:5–10)

Give Attention

My son, give attention to my words; incline your ear to my sayings. Do not let them depart from your eyes; keep them in the midst of your heart; for they are life to those who find them, and health to all their flesh. Keep your heart with all diligence, for out of it spring the issues of life. Put away from you a deceitful mouth, and put perverse lips far from you. Let your eyes look straight ahead, and your eyelids look right before you. Ponder the path of your feet, and let all your ways be established. Do not turn to the right or the left; remove your foot from evil.

(Proverbs 4:20–27)

The Words of Your Mouth

You are snared by the words of your own mouth; you are taken by the words of your mouth.

(Proverbs 6:2)

Fill Their Treasuries

Riches and honor are with me, enduring riches and righteousness. My fruit is better than gold, yes, than fine gold, and my revenue than choice silver. I traverse the way of righteousness, in the midst of the paths of justice, that I may cause those who love me to inherit wealth, that I may fill their treasuries. (Proverbs 8:18–21)

Favor from the Lord

Blessed is the man who listens to me, watching daily at my gates, waiting at the posts of my doors. For whoever finds me finds life, and obtains favor from the LORD. (Proverbs 8:34–35)

Memory of the Righteous Is Blessed

Blessings are on the head of the righteous, but violence covers the mouth of the wicked. The memory of the righteous is blessed, but the name of the wicked will rot. (Proverbs 10:6–7)

Blessing of the Lord

The blessing of the LORD makes one rich, and He adds no sorrow with it. (Proverbs 10:22)

A Good Man

A good man leaves an inheritance to his children's children, but the wealth of the sinner is stored up for the righteous. (Proverbs 13:22)

Your Plans Be Established and Succeed

Roll your works upon the Lord [commit and trust them wholly to Him; He will cause your thoughts to become agreeable to His will, and] so shall your plans be established and succeed.

(Proverbs 16:3 AMP)

Merry Heart

A merry heart does good, like medicine, but a broken spirit dries the bones.   (Proverbs 17:22)

The Lord Is a Strong Tower

The name of the LORD is a strong tower; the righteous run to it and are safe.   (Proverbs 18:10)

The Power of the Tongue

Death and life are in the power of the tongue, and those who love it will eat its fruit.

(Proverbs 18:21)

Train a Child

Train up a child in the way he should go, and when he is old he will not depart from it.

(Proverbs 22:6)

Shall Prosper

Blessed is the man who walks not in the counsel of the ungodly, nor stands in the path of sinners, nor sits in the seat of the scornful; but his delight is in the law of the LORD, and in His law he meditates day and night. He shall be like a tree planted by the rivers of water, that brings forth its fruit in its season, whose leaf also shall not wither; and whatever he does shall prosper.   (Psalm 1:1–3)

My Shepherd

The LORD is my shepherd; I shall not want. He makes me to lie down in green pastures; He leads me beside the still waters. He restores my soul; He leads me in the paths of righteousness for His name's sake. Yea, though I walk through the valley of the shadow of death, I will fear no evil; for You are with me; Your rod and Your staff, they comfort me. You prepare a table before me in the presence of my enemies; You anoint my head with oil; my cup runs over. Surely goodness and mercy shall follow me all the days of my life; and I will dwell in the house of the LORD forever.   (Psalm 23)

You Healed Me

O LORD my God, I cried out to You, and You healed me.   (Psalm 30:2)

Delivered Me from All My Fears

I sought the LORD, and He heard me, and delivered me from all my fears.   (Psalm 34:4)

Angel Encamps All Around

The angel of the LORD encamps all around those who fear Him, and delivers them.   (Psalm 34:7)

The Man Who Trusts in Him

Oh, taste and see that the LORD is good; blessed is the man who trusts in Him!   (Psalm 34:8)

Any Good Thing

The young lions lack and suffer hunger; but those who seek the LORD shall not lack any good thing.   (Psalm 34:10)

Prosperity

Let them shout for joy and be glad, who favor my righteous cause; and let them say continually, "Let the LORD be magnified, who has pleasure in the prosperity of His servant."   (Psalm 35:27)

Lord Upholds Him with His Hand

The steps of a good man are ordered by the LORD, and He delights in his way. Though he fall, he shall not be utterly cast down; for the LORD upholds him with His hand.   (Psalm 37:23–24)

His Descendants Are Blessed

I have been young, and now am old; yet I have not seen the righteous forsaken, nor his descendants begging bread. He is ever merciful, and lends; and his descendants are blessed.   (Psalm 37:25–26)

We Will Not Fear

God is our refuge and strength, a very present help in trouble. Therefore we will not fear, even though the earth be removed, and though the mountains be carried into the midst of the sea; though its waters roar and be troubled, though the mountains shake with its swelling. Selah (Psalm 46:1–3)

Be Still

Be still, and know that I am God; I will be exalted among the nations, I will be exalted in the earth!
(Psalm 46:10)

I Will Deliver You

Call upon Me in the day of trouble; I will deliver you, and you shall glorify Me.   (Psalm 50:15)

God Is for Me

The very day I call for help, the tide of battle turns. My enemies flee! This one thing I know: God is for me! I am trusting God—oh, praise his promises! I am not afraid of anything mere man can do to me! Yes, praise his promises.   (Psalm 56:9–11 TLB)

Daily Loads Us with Benefits

Blessed be the Lord, who daily loads us with benefits, the God of our salvation! Selah (Psalm 68:19)

God of Miracles

You are the God of miracles and wonders! You still demonstrate your awesome power.
(Psalm 77:14 TLB)

No Good Thing Will He Withhold

For the LORD God is a sun and shield; the LORD will give grace and glory; no good thing will He withhold from those who walk uprightly. (Psalm 84:11)

There Is No Unrighteousness in Him

The righteous shall flourish like a palm tree, he shall grow like a cedar in Lebanon. Those who are planted in the house of the LORD shall flourish in the courts of our God. They shall still bear fruit in old age; they shall be fresh and flourishing, To declare that the LORD is upright; He is my rock, and there is no unrighteousness in Him. (Psalm 92:12–15)

Healed

He sent His word and healed them, and delivered them from their destructions. (Psalm 107:20)

Precious

Precious in the sight of the LORD is the death of His saints. (Psalm 116:15)

I Shall Not Die, but Live

I shall not die, but live, and declare the works of the LORD. (Psalm 118:17)

Faithfulness Endures to All Generations

Forever, O LORD, Your word is settled in heaven. Your faithfulness endures to all generations; You established the earth, and it abides. They continue this day according to Your ordinances, for all are Your servants. (Psalm 119:89–91)

Light to My Path

Your word is a lamp to my feet and a light to my path. (Psalm 119:105)

The Beginning and the End

"I am the Alpha and the Omega, the Beginning and the End," says the Lord, "who is and who was and who is to come, the Almighty." (Revelation 1:8)

I Am Alive Forevermore

Do not be afraid; I am the First and the Last. I am He who lives, and was dead, and behold, I am alive forevermore. Amen. And I have the keys of Hades and of Death. (Revelation 1:17–18)

Have Kept My Word

See, I have set before you an open door, and no one can shut it; for you have a little strength, have kept My word, and have not denied My name. (Revelation 3:8)

I Will Come In to Him

Behold, I stand at the door and knock. If anyone hears My voice and opens the door, I will come in to him and dine with him, and he with Me. (Revelation 3:20)

Behold, I Make All Things New

"And God will wipe away every tear from their eyes; there shall be no more death, nor sorrow, nor crying. There shall be no more pain, for the former things have passed away." Then He who sat on the throne said, "Behold, I make all things new." And He said to me, "Write, for these words are true and faithful." (Revelation 21:4–5)

The Just Shall Live by Faith

For I am not ashamed of the gospel of Christ, for it is the power of God to salvation for everyone who believes, for the Jew first and also for the Greek. For in it the righteousness of God is revealed from faith to faith; as it is written, "The just shall live by faith." (Romans 1:16)

So Shall Your Descendants Be

God, who gives life to the dead and calls those things which do not exist as though they did; who, contrary to hope, in hope believed, so that [Abraham] became the father of many nations, according to what was spoken, "So shall your descendants be." (Romans 4:17–18)

Peace with God

Therefore, having been justified by faith, we have peace with God through our Lord Jesus Christ. (Romans 5:1)

Christ Died for Us

But God demonstrates His own love toward us, in that while we were still sinners, Christ died for us.
(Romans 5:8)

Gift of God

But now having been set free from sin, and having become slaves of God, you have your fruit to holiness, and the end, everlasting life. For the wages of sin is death, but the gift of God is eternal life in Christ Jesus our Lord.
(Romans 6:22–23)

Free from the Law of Sin and Death

There is therefore now no condemnation to those who are in Christ Jesus, who do not walk according to the flesh, but according to the Spirit. For the law of the Spirit of life in Christ Jesus has made me free from the law of sin and death.
(Romans 8:1–2)

All Things Work Together for Good

And we know that all things work together for good to those who love God, to those who are the called according to His purpose.
(Romans 8:28)

God Is for Us

If God is for us, who can be against us?
(Romans 8:31)

Separate Us from the Love of God

Who shall separate us from the love of Christ? Shall tribulation, or distress, or persecution, or famine, or nakedness, or peril, or sword? As it is written: "For Your sake we are killed all day long; we are accounted as sheep for the slaughter." Yet in all these things we are more than conquerors through Him who loved us. For I am persuaded that neither death nor life, nor angels nor principalities nor powers, nor things present nor things to come, nor height nor depth, nor any other created thing, shall be able to separate us from the love of God which is in Christ Jesus our Lord.   (Romans 8:35–39)

Never Go Back on His Promise

For God's gifts and his call can never be withdrawn; he will never go back on his promises.
(Romans 11:29 TLB)

Acceptable to God

For the kingdom of God is not eating and drinking, but righteousness and peace and joy in the Holy Spirit. For he who serves Christ in these things is acceptable to God and approved by men.
(Romans 14:17–18)

Not from Faith

Whatever is not from faith is sin.   (Romans 14:23)

The Battle Is the Lord's

For the battle is the Lord's, and He will give you into our hands.   (1 Samuel 17:47)

We Shall Be with the Lord

For the Lord Himself will descend from heaven with a shout, with the voice of an archangel, and with the trumpet of God. And the dead in Christ will rise first. Then we who are alive and remain shall be caught up together with them in the clouds to meet the Lord in the air. And thus we shall always be with the Lord. (1 Thessalonians 4:16–17)

Faithful Is He

He who calls you is faithful, who also will do it. (1 Thessalonians 5:24)

Power, Love, and a Sound Mind

For God has not given us a spirit of fear, but of power and of love and of a sound mind. (2 Timothy 1:7)

Thoroughly Equipped for Good Work

All Scripture is given by inspiration of God, and is profitable for doctrine, for reproof, for correction, for instruction in righteousness, that the man of God may be complete, thoroughly equipped for every good work. (2 Timothy 3:16–17)

By My Spirit

"Not by might nor by power, but by My Spirit," says the LORD of hosts. (Zechariah 4:6)

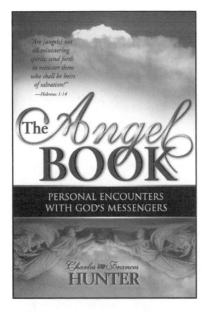

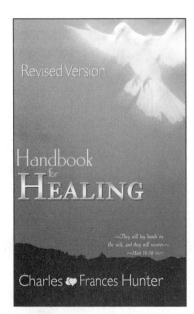